THE UK MEDIA LAW POCKETBOOK

As media law becomes more complicated and some of the leading textbooks thicker and larger, this concise guide provides core information without patronizing those with existing knowledge or bamboozling those with little expertise.

Suitable for journalists, media workers, and anyone in the cultural or publishing industries, the book engages and addresses the Internet and blogging, social networking, instant messaging, digital multi-media publication and consumption as well as traditional print and broadcast.

Each chapter covers substantive 'black letter law' and regulation/ethics, and kept in mind throughout is the difference in duties and obligations between words and pictures, print and broadcasting.

The focus is on the law relating to England and Wales, but with references to key differences to bear in mind in Scotland and Northern Ireland.

Chapters start with bullet points, then flesh out the details and summarize pitfalls to avoid. Readers are left in no doubt about liabilities and potential penalties.

Anticipating a dynamically changing arena, the text is also backed up by downloadable sound podcasts, video-casts, Internet source links throughout the book text, and a companion website so that any significant updates are immediately accessible direct from the ebook.

For additional resources visit the companion website at www.routledge.com/textbooks/crook

Tim Crook LLB is Senior Lecturer and Head of Radio at Goldsmiths, University of London. He has worked professionally in radio, theatre, television and film as a journalist, producer, director and sound designer for more than 30 years. Throughout this period he has taught media law and ethics to professional journalists and students at all levels. He is the author of *The Sound Handbook* (2011), *Comparative Media Law and Ethics* (2009), *Radio Drama: Theory and Practice* (1999), and *International Radio Journalism: History, Theory and Practice* (1997).

UK MEDIA LAW POCKETBOOK COMPANION WEBSITE

The companion website for the book can be accessed here: www.routledge.com/textbooks/crook

The companion web-site updates the topics for each chapter and provides an online link to all the sound podcasts and video-casts. There are additional resources that complement the book. For example a short guide on how to use UK Freedom of Information law, and advice about the risks of using social media for gossip, rumour and opinion.

THE UK MEDIA LAW POCKETBOOK

by Tim Crook

Published by Routledge March 2013

Introduction

Explains the mission of the book in being a print, ebook, and multimedia nexus. UK media law is explained in terms of primary (legislation and case law) and secondary (regulation and self-regulation in terms of Ofcom, BBC Editorial Guidelines and independent press regulation after the Leveson Inquiry report and replacing the Press Complaints Commission) Recommendations for more detailed follow-up in terms of bibliography. Explaining the legalised nature of professional media research, information gathering and publication, and the consequences of making mistakes in terms of criminal prosecution, civil litigation, disciplinary action by employers, regulatory reprimand, fines, suspension and cancellation of broadcasting licences. The introduction explains the transition position of the new Defamation Bill becoming an Act of Parliament between 2012-13 and the likely shape of new independent regulation of the print media with powers to fine up to £1 million, order prominent corrections and apologies for breaching a constantly evolving code of ethics.

THE UK MEDIA LAW POCKETBOOK

Tim Crook

LONDON AND NEW YORK

First published 2013
by Routledge
2 Park Square, Milton Park, Abingdon, Oxon OX14 4RN

Simultaneously published in the USA and Canada
by Routledge
711 Third Avenue, New York, NY 10017

Routledge is an imprint of the Taylor & Francis Group, an informa business

British Library Cataloguing in Publication Data
A catalogue record for this book is available from the British Library

Library of Congress Cataloging in Publication Data
Crook, Tim, 1959–
The UK media law pocketbook / by Tim Crook
  pages cm
  Includes bibliographical references and index
  1. Press law--Great Britain. I. Title
  KD2875.C76 2013   343.4109'98--dc23
  2012037095

ISBN: 978-0-415-64523-2 (hbk)
ISBN: 978-0-415-64524-9 (pbk)
ISBN: 978-0-203-07846-4 (ebk)

Typeset in Baskerville and Scala Sans
by Bookcraft Ltd, Stroud, Gloucestershire

CONTENTS

CONTENTS

INTRODUCTION

This book is intended to be a concise, short, and clear quick guide to media law affecting anyone working in the UK. It comes with a companion website that updates an unstable and quickly changing area of the law and includes sound podcasts and video-casts. It is designed to work for people in traditional print, broadcast or online multi-media. There are direct links to more information and key sources.

A downloadable sound file on the introduction that seeks to explain the purpose and mission of the book.
https://soundcloud.com/comparativemedialaw/
introduction-uk-media-law

You need to know about—
Primary media law: legislation and case law (ruling by courts) in this country and Europe, which when transgressed can result in criminal prosecution and penalties (fine and/or imprisonment) and/or civil litigation (astronomical legal costs and damages); and

Secondary media law: 'ethics' and regulation.

If you breach these 'professional standards' you might find yourself subject to disciplinary warnings or dismissal from work (particularly where your duty to comply with a professional ethics code is written into your employment contract) and/or fines, suspension or removal of broadcast licences, and damaging public adjudications for your employer publisher.

Primary and secondary media law overlap. Sometimes it is different if you are working in broadcasting (BBC or independent broadcasting) and print/online. In UK broadcasting obeying statutory regulatory law is known as 'compliance'. This means that the working broadcaster has to deal with two levels of control. At the BBC, primary legal matters are supervised by a team of specialist lawyers in 'Programme Legal Advice'. What I call 'secondary media law', but in the BBC is described as 'Editorial Guidelines', is under the control of a separate supervisory infrastructure called 'Editorial Policy and Standards'. Essentially the difference between what were regarded as media law and media ethics is anachronistic, out of date and redundant. What were previously regarded as journalistic ethics have been sucked into the category of 'secondary media law' obligation because section 12 of the Human Rights Act 1998 gave the courts the power to take into account journalistic codes of ethics when balancing legal disputes involving Article 10 Freedom of Expression and Article 8 Privacy.

Obviously any ethical discretion on the part of an individual journalist ceases to be so when it becomes subject to investigation, adjudication and punishment – which is the case with Ofcom in statutory penalties imposed on broadcast licensees (the employers) and disciplinary action by the BBC against its employees and contractors in failing to observe 'the Guidelines'. A new independent regulator for UK print media (newspapers and magazines and associated online publication) is to have the power to impose financial sanctions up to 1% of turnover, with a maximum of £1 million for serious or systematic breaches of a revamped and developed ethics/standards code, which until the end of 2012 was previously regulated by the Press Complaints Commission (PCC). It is expected that the new regulator will have the power to require publication of corrections in disputes over accuracy and the publication of apologies for breaches of other ethical rules. The new regulator will inherit the previous PCC case law and all its resources and *The Editors' Codebook* referenced in this book will be edited and updated to serve the succeeding body.

As if the landscape of media law and regulation for the British multi-media journalist was not complicated enough, you need to know that the BBC and Ofcom overlap in most areas of secondary media law (broadcast content regulation) except in relation to due impartiality, due accuracy and undue prominence of views and opinions, elections and referendums, and commercial references in television programming. The BBC has an editorial complaints infrastructure operated by the BBC Trust that is independent from Ofcom and carries out its own enquiries and publishes its own adjudications. And yes it does mean that both BBC and Ofcom investigate and adjudicate on the same programmes, complaints and issues.

The Westminster Parliament is processing a new Defamation Bill. I have done my best to anticipate this in the book's content, and will continue to do so via the companion website and articulate clarity on the outcome of these legislative, political and industrial narratives.

It is my belief that professional media practice and journalism in the UK has become increasingly 'legalized' in the sense that so much conduct and content requires supervision, advice and permission from lawyers and then the issue of whether it has transgressed primary and secondary media law is decided by state officials in the form of prosecutors and judges. Journalism is being codified and defined by state legislature, executive and judiciary as to what is permissible so long as it fulfils the criteria of being 'responsible'. Everything else is potentially 'irresponsible' and therefore unlawful.

In the larger broadcast media organizations in-house lawyers participate in editorial meetings and are present during editing and live transmission. They have a permanent role in the editorial infrastructure. At the BBC journalists have to comply with what are known as 'mandatory referrals' to 'Director of Editorial

Policy' and/or 'Programme Legal Advice'. Since so much of what a journalist and professional media communicator does is in legal jeopardy, my advice would be to ensure that you individually have a documentary and evidential trail of permission, direction and agreement to your conduct and content creation. Keep copious notes and all emails, and file these separately from your work computer systems.

If you are freelance, a single author publisher, or part of a smaller media outlet with limited resources, you are entitled to feel that your situation is somewhat perilous. Self-censorship and excessive caution are often the only means of survival. Even the UK's National Union of Journalists recommends buying into a media law insurance policy that at its lower scale can add several hundred pounds to your annual professional costs.

Bear in mind that if you are sent abroad to carry out reporting and media assignments you will be subject to the law pertaining to the foreign jurisdiction you are operating in. *International Libel & Privacy Handbook*, edited by Charles J. Glasser Jr., with 2nd edition published in 2010 by Bloomberg Press, USA, may be of assistance. A simple explanation for why care needs to be taken is that recording research conversations on your phone without telling the other side, even for note-taking purposes, is a criminal offence in Germany, but not so in the UK. Even in the USA with its constitutional First Amendment, there are 11 states, namely California, Connecticut, Florida, Illinois, Maryland, Massachusetts, Montana, Nevada, New Hampshire, Pennsylvania and Washington, that require all parties to consent when one party wants to record a telephone conversation.

At the time of writing the number of journalists and professional media communicators in the UK was in decline, perhaps due to economic recession. The BBC employed less than 17,000 people and an estimated 7,000 worked as 'journalists'. There are no clear and reliable figures on the total number of 'journalists' employed in all media sectors throughout the country, but taking into account the trend in redundancy a vague estimate could be 40,000 and declining. I would advise anyone employed in this area to be a member of a professional trade union or organization. This is because bodies such as the Chartered Institute of Journalists (1,500 members, http://cioj.co.uk/) and the National Union of Journalists (38,000 members, http://www.nuj.org.uk/) provide a legal advice service to their members and will represent them in employment law matters. The CIoJ and NUJ are also very good at providing training and career development resources.

Online sites beyond my control can change their links without notice. So I cannot guarantee consistency, certainty and clarity by so many of the authorities that control and impact on you as media communicators. You might be able to find the resource again using a search engine, or the resource might have been withdrawn.

For more detail on the subject I make these recommendations:

Essential Law for Journalists, 21st edition 2012 by Mark Hanna and Mike Dodd, published by Oxford University Press;
Journalism Law by Francis Quinn, 3rd edition 2011, published by Pearson;
The Editors' Codebook by Ian Beales, 2011 edition (or latest), published by the Press Standards Board of Finance Ltd.

I apologize for immodestly recommending my book *Comparative Media Law and Ethics* published by Routledge in 2009 and its companion website http://www.ma-radio.gold.ac.uk/cmle if you want a text that investigates UK media law in its international context, particularly the USA and discusses the whys and hows as much as the whats.

Ethics for Journalists by Richard Keeble (2nd edn 2008) also published by Routledge, and *Journalism Ethics and Regulation* by Chris Frost (3rd edn in 2011) published by Pearson Longman, and *The Ethical Journalist* by Tony Harcup (2006) are useful discursive texts on the morality of journalism. For a substantial and effective explanation of British government, power and the country's public institutions I recommend the latest edition of *Essential Public Affairs for Journalists* by James Morrison, 2nd edition 2011, published by Oxford University Press, and in my opinion the best guide on professional reporting techniques is *Essential Reporting: The NCTJ Guide for Trainee Journalists* by Jon Smith, 2011, published by Sage. I particularly recommend chapter 14 on 'Court Reporting'.

The Press Association's *Media Lawyer* edited by Mike Dodd in 'newsletter' published bimonthly and its excellent website is well worth subscribing to should you wish to be kept up to date with the never-ending changes and developments in British media law.

I admire and respect everybody else who has written books on journalism, media law and ethics and could not recommend them more highly. If I fail in my mission set out in the first sentence, it is all my fault and I apologize unreservedly.

I thank everyone who has put up with me in work, home and personal life and in particular, helped me learn my subject, teach it and write about it.

MEDIA CONTEMPT AND REPORTING CRIME

Key professional rules for reporting crime and covering criminal proceedings:

- Laws that control communication to protect the right to fair trial (Article 6 of the European Convention on Human Rights (ECHR)) and the administration of justice meaning criminal enquiries, litigation and legal proceedings at all levels
- Key issues to remember: substantial risk (timing and scale of publication) of serious prejudice (content of publication) or impeding justice (disruption/impact on enquiry) applying from the time of arrest
- Successful prosecution of the *Daily Mirror* and *The Sun* for vilification of retired teacher Chris Jefferies who was an exonerated suspect in the murder enquiry of Joanna Yeates
- Successful prosecution of the *Daily Mail* and *The Sun* for publishing online prejudicial images of a defendant

during the trial that were not seen by the jury and removed shortly after publication

- Successful prosecution of the *Spectator* weekly magazine for prejudicial editorial column at the beginning of a murder trial and while postponing reporting bans were in force
- Successful prosecution of the *Daily Mirror* and *Daily Mail* for publishing background in trial of Levi Bellfield for murdering Milly Dowler when jury were deliberating on a lesser charge for an offence against another victim
- Analysing substantial risk (fade factor – size of audience and timing) and serious prejudice (nature of content). The first test case: the man who walked into the Queen's bedroom
- Successful prosecutions of one juror for online research and communicating to an acquitted defendant on Facebook, and another for online research into the background and previous criminal trial of a defendant despite being ordered not to do so by the trial judges
- Defying directions or orders of the court is a contempt of court whether the order is right in law or not
- Judges can issue orders and injunctions removing archive articles online and postponing publication of articles and broadcast of programmes if there is deemed to be a substantial risk of serious prejudice to forthcoming or concurrent jury trials
- Cross-jurisdictional reach. If you publish outside the UK, but your publications can be read, seen and heard in the UK, you can arguably still be liable
- Although parliamentarians and foreign publications appear to have immunity from contempt prosecution, this does not necessarily extend to anyone reporting the information that is injuncted/banned/interdicted (that's the term used in Scotland) or likely to be a serious prejudice or impedance to the administration of justice

- Relatives or friends of persons convicted of crime should not generally be identified without their consent, unless genuinely relevant to the story and particular regard should be paid to the potentially vulnerable position of children who witness, or are victims of, crime
- No payment or offer of a payment to a witness – or any person who may reasonably be expected to be called as a witness – should be made in 'active' criminal cases (after arrest etc) until the suspect has been freed unconditionally without charge or bail, proceedings have been discontinued, a guilty plea has been entered and accepted, or announcement of not guilty verdict
- The payment to witness rule also applies when legal proceedings are likely and foreseeable, and any payment to a witness later cited to give evidence in criminal cases must be disclosed to the prosecution and defence, with the witness being advised of this obligation. This ethical rule is subject to a public interest justification
- Payment or offers of payment for stories, pictures or information that seek to exploit a particular crime or to glorify or glamorize crime in general must not be made directly or via agents to convicted or confessed criminals or to their associates – who may include family, friends and colleagues. This is subject to public interest but when invoked, the editors need to demonstrate good reasons
- Broadcasters (radio and television) must not include material that is likely to encourage or incite the commissioning of crime or to lead to disorder, and descriptions or demonstrations of criminal techniques which contain essential details that can enable the commission of crime must not be transmitted unless editorially justified
- Journalists must avoid publishing material that could put people's lives in danger or prejudice inquiries into hijacks or kidnappings (regulatory requirement for broadcasters). All journalists, whether print, online or

broadcast, should cooperate with police requests for news 'blackouts' aimed at saving a victim's life. Any coverage of anti-terrorist or hostage recovery events must not include live material that would help assailants counter armed police or anti-terrorist operations

✭ A downloadable sound file of these 'bullet points' on media contempt and reporting crime.
1.0 podcast downloadable https://soundcloud.com/comparativemedialaw/chapter-1-bullet-points-uk

A short video-cast explaining key UK media law points on media contempt and reporting crime
1. video-cast http://youtu.be/9jW78STg5KY

1.1 BALANCING FREEDOM OF EXPRESSION WITH THE INDIVIDUAL'S RIGHT TO A FAIR TRIAL

The UK legal system balances the right of the media to report its proceedings, known as 'open justice' with the right of a person to have a fair trial, which is enshrined in Schedule 1, Article 6 of the Human Rights Act 1998 (HRA) derived from Article 6 of the ECHR:

Article 6 Right to a fair trial:

1 In the determination of his civil rights and obligations or of any criminal charge against him, everyone is entitled to a fair and public hearing within a reasonable time by an independent and impartial tribunal established by law. Judgment shall be pronounced publicly but the press and public may be excluded from all or part of the trial in the interest of morals, public order or national security in a democratic society, where the interests of juveniles or the

protection of the private life of the parties so require, or to the extent strictly necessary in the opinion of the court in special circumstances where publicity would prejudice the interests of justice.

2   Everyone charged with a criminal offence shall be presumed innocent until proved guilty according to law.

3   Everyone charged with a criminal offence has the following minimum rights:

   a   to be informed promptly, in a language which he understands and in detail, of the nature and cause of the accusation against him;

   b   to have adequate time and facilities for the preparation of his defence;

   c   to defend himself in person or through legal assistance of his own choosing or, if he has not sufficient means to pay for legal assistance, to be given it free when the interests of justice so require;

   d   to examine or have examined witnesses against him and to obtain the attendance and examination of witnesses on his behalf under the same conditions as witnesses against him;

   e   to have the free assistance of an interpreter if he cannot understand or speak the language used in court.

When reporting people accused of crime you have an ethical obligation to uphold the principles of accuracy, avoid privacy intrusion and harassment, and must not publish anything that could lead to the identification of sexual assault victims. Furthermore, you must avoid identifying innocent relatives or friends who are not relevant to the story, whose relationship is not in the public domain, and where it is not in the public interest to identify them. The PCC upheld a complaint against the *Evening Standard* in 2005 when it wrongly alleged that an Islamic bookshop near Baker Street in London stocked extremist literature and DVDs. The report was published in the aftermath of the July 7 suicide bombings and the PCC said: 'the consequences of the misleading allegations

– particularly given the fact that the shop's contact details had been prominently displayed – could have been extremely serious for the complainant'.

Human Rights Act 1998
http://www.legislation.gov.uk/ukpga/1998/42/contents
See PCC ruling: Samir El-Atar v *Evening Standard* (Report 72, 2005)
http://www.pcc.org.uk/news/index.html?article=MjE3Mw

✴   A downloadable sound file of this section about balancing media freedom with the right to a fair trial.
    1.1 podcast downloadable https://soundcloud.com/comparativemedialaw/podcast1-1-the-uk-media-law

1.2   EXPLAINING MEDIA CONTEMPT

Statutory contempt (an offence created by an Act of Parliament, in this case the 1981 Contempt of Court Act) is publishing information that creates a substantial risk of serious prejudice, or impedes the administration of justice. Prosecution under section 83 of the Criminal Justice Act 2003 for breaching media court orders can be by summary process, e.g. at magistrates' court level only, where maximum jail sentence is six months and fine is limited to £5,000. The criminal sanctions on conviction for an offence under the 1981 Contempt of Court Act include an unlimited fine and/or maximum jail sentence of two years' imprisonment. These are 'strict liability offences' which means that lack of intention is no defence. Cases can only be prosecuted by the Attorney General, one of the government's law officers, a politician and usually an experienced lawyer such as a senior solicitor (lawyer who tends to advise and prepare litigation) or court advocate (known as barristers or QCs (Queen's Counsel)).

Office of UK Attorney General
http://www.attorneygeneral.gov.uk/Pages/default.aspx

Media contempt as a crime is usually triable before a judicial panel of three or two judges in the Divisional Court of the English High Court (Administrative division) in London, though the *Spectator* case in 2012 indicates there is now an option for summary prosecution before a District Judge in the magistrates' court under section 83 of the Criminal Justice Act 2003. In Scotland proceedings would be held before the High Court of Justiciary. The crime has to be proved beyond reasonable doubt.

There is an offence of contempt under common law (an offence created by judge-made case law/precedent and historical custom and practice). Unlike the statutory form of the crime, the Attorney General has to prove intention. Campaigning newspapers, websites, bloggers and broadcast programmes with a partial position could be liable under common law contempt if there is a provable intention to prejudice a future trial at any stage of a civil or criminal case (even before an individual has been arrested), and the emotional, political, potentially malicious and partial nature of the publication becomes evidence of intention.

Under the 1981 Contempt of Court Act, the strict liability rule applies from the time a case is active. This is once someone has been arrested for a crime, or a warrant has been issued for arrest, issuing of a summons, oral charging, or when a civil case is set down for trial. The contempt risk in civil cases is usually only relevant to libel, false imprisonment and malicious prosecution cases sitting with juries. A case remains active until proceedings are over. A notice to appeal against conviction and sentence after a jury trial is not usually considered to be a continuation of the proceedings or the activation of a new media contempt risk. This is because it has rarely been admitted by the judiciary that professional judges are susceptible to seriously prejudicial coverage. The situation may not be the case with lay magistrates though the issue has not been tested.

Matters deemed to create a substantial risk of serious prejudice and impedance to the administration of justice could include (on the basis of previous prosecutions):

a   publishing previous convictions or acquittals;

b   suggesting an accused person(s) has confessed;

c   suggesting accusations of more serious crime or crimes than the accused persons are facing;

d   suggesting accused people are guilty;

e   saying something so bad about them that you could prejudice a potential juror against them;

f   publishing photographs or sketches of the accused when identification is likely to be a contested issue at a future trial, or images that visually communicate seriously prejudicial information about the accused;

g   publishing information that disrupts or disables a police enquiry and/or defence case by preventing the collection of critical evidence e.g. discouraging witnesses from coming forward to tell the truth or catastrophically discrediting or invalidating their evidence.

The legal concept of media contempt and the extent of liability for media communicators has a wider remit. The Director of Public Prosecutions (DPP) and Crown Prosecution Service (CPS) for England and Wales discussed 'quasi-contempt' as also including the breach of statutory restrictions on the reporting of proceedings which are treated as substantive criminal offences. These include:

- sections 39 and 49 Children and Young Persons Act 1933 – prohibition on publication of a name, address or school calculated to identify a child;
- section 8 Magistrates' Courts Act 1980 – Restrictions on reports of committal proceedings;
- section 5 Sexual Offences (Amendment) Act 1992 – prohibiting publication of details that identify a victim of rape or other serious sexual offence who has anonymity.

Crown Prosecution Service resources on 'Contempt of Court and Reporting Restrictions'
http://www.cps.gov.uk/legal/a_to_c/contempt_of_court/index.html

✳   A downloadable sound file of this section explaining media
    contempt.
    1.2 podcast downloadable https://soundcloud.com/
    comparativemedialaw/podcast1-2-uk-media-law

1.3 GOVERNMENT AND JUDICIAL POLICY ON TOLERATION OF MEDIA COVERAGE OF POLICE ENQUIRIES AND COURT PROCEEDINGS CHANGING

Dominic Grieve QC was appointed Attorney General in the coalition government elected in 2010 and he has shown a determination
to apply the 'strict liability rule' set out in section 2(2) of the 1981
Contempt of Court Act against media publications that create a
'substantial risk that the course of justice in the proceedings in
question will be seriously impeded or prejudiced'. Mr Grieve has
elevated the significance of the phrase 'seriously impeded' when
up until now most media lawyers and case histories have focused
on the idea of the publications 'seriously prejudicing' the minds of
lay jurors.

New case law in 2011/12 has developed and reinforced the additional obligation to avoid 'impeding' the administration of justice
by demonizing or 'monstering' a suspect through critical depiction
of a suspect's character/personality to the extent that other equally
significant suspect(s) will not be investigated and the defence case
and police enquiry will be diverted/undermined or adversely
affected. There is an increasing tendency for judges to issue injunctions and orders against publications that could be deemed to
generate serious prejudice either before or during jury criminal
trials and this can lead to the removal of archive news articles and
the suspension of broadcasts and publications.

Up until 2010 the 28-day detention period in terrorist cases
lengthening the period between arrest and charge, combined
with the intensity of 24/7 media coverage, appeared to shift the
observance of the strict liability rule to the time when a charge was
made, or even the first court appearance. This trend was encouraged by the recognition of the 'fade factor' between intense media

coverage of the crime, arrest, charge and first court appearance and eventual trial. A gap of several months, sometimes a year or more, was considered to lead to a 'fade of memory' in the minds of potential jurors who were likely to try the case at the Crown Court.

This situation was encouraged by the lack of prosecutions by previous Attorneys General when the 1981 Contempt of Court Act seemed to be observed more in its breach than its compliance. But several prosecutions taken since the election of the Conservative and Liberal Democrat coalition in 2010, and the appointment of Dominic Grieve QC as Attorney General, have indicated a change in policy to encourage observance of the rule from the time of arrest.

Mr Grieve has explained that he was responding to a tendency for the UK media to push the boundaries. It was his view that on occasion the press had lost any sense of internal constraint and felt able, indeed entitled, to print what they wished, shielded by the right of 'freedom of expression' without any of the associated responsibilities.

Attorney General's speech to City University. 'Contempt: A Balancing Act'
http://www.attorneygeneral.gov.uk/NewsCentre/Speeches/Pages/ContemptAbalancingact.asp

---

There is a defence under section 5 of the 1981 Contempt of Court Act to protect publications on matters of public interest about subjects that are 'merely incidental' to ongoing trials and proceedings, but recent case histories indicate courts tend to err on the side of caution in issuing injunctions and orders to postpone publication/transmission and the removal of archive online articles. In July 2012, Mr Justice Flaux at Birmingham Crown Court made an order under section 45 of the Senior Courts Act 1981 postponing the BBC's transmission of two documentaries about the summer riots of the previous year while presiding over the trial of eight defendants later acquitted in relation to the deaths of three men run over by a car. Also in 2012 Mr Justice Fulford directed that online background reports on PC Simon Harwood, later acquitted of the manslaughter of Ian Tomlinson at Southwark Crown Court, should be temporarily removed until the end of the proceedings. In 2012 the Law Commission for England and Wales announced its research project and consultation on law reform of UK media contempt law in the new age of the Internet, blogging and social media. It was tabling a statutory power for judges and courts to order the removal of online news articles deemed to be prejudicial to active court cases.

The Law Commission of England and Wales consultation on reform of contempt law
http://lawcommission.justice.gov.uk/consultations/contempt.htm

---

1.3.1   REPORTING COURT CASES: SOME SIMPLE GROUND RULES

a   Never report anything said in the absence of the jury until after all the verdicts have been returned.

b   Stick to reporting accurately what is said in court and do not paraphrase using 'sexier' and more sensationalist language.

c   Make sure your reports are fair and accurate. To be fair involves putting the other side of the story. Accuracy speaks for itself.

d   Find out about any existing court reporting restrictions, in particular orders under sections 4(2) and 11 of the 1981 Contempt of Court Act as well as any other legislation. If you think it is possible that an order might be in place speak to the court clerk, and/or contact the legal adviser and relevant Court Service administrator at the court centre. See Chapter 2 for a more detailed guide on reporting the courts.

★   A downloadable sound file of this section on the stricter approach to fair trial/free media laws in the UK.
1.3 podcast downloadable https://soundcloud.com/comparativemedialaw/podcast1-3-uk-media-law

1.4 SUCCESSFUL PROSECUTION OF NATIONAL NEWSPAPERS WHO VILIFIED AN INNOCENT SUSPECT IN MURDER ENQUIRY

On 29 July 2011 the Lord Chief Justice, Lord Igor Judge, ruled that *The Sun* and *Daily Mirror* newspapers had committed media contempt by vilifying the reputation of retired teacher Christopher Jefferies after his arrest during the enquiry into the murder of Joanna Yeates in Bristol at the end of 2010 and beginning of the New Year 2011. Vincent Tabak was subsequently convicted of Joanna's murder. Mr Jefferies was an entirely innocent man. The case generates the legal principle that 'the vilification of a suspect under arrest' can be a potential impedimenta to the course of justice.

The Sun reported 'he was a stalker, with an obsession with death, who let himself into the flats of other occupants of the building where Miss Yeates lived, and that he had an unhealthy interest in blonde young women'. The judge said the *Daily Mirror* had published two articles with the headlines on the front page declaring: 'Jo suspect is peeping Tom', 'Arrest landlord spied on flat couple', 'Friend in jail for paedophile crimes', 'Cops now probe 36-years old murder'. The ruling observed: 'while positively asserting that Mr Jefferies was a voyeur, without directly asserting that he was involved in paedophile crimes or a long unresolved murder, the impression conveyed to an objective reader was that he was somehow linked with not one but two awful, additional crimes'.

The Lord Chief Justice added these articles vilified Mr Jefferies long before the fade factor could have begun to operate, and 'the risks to the preparation of his defence would have been serious'. The court imposed fines of £18,000 on *The Sun* and £50,000 on the *Daily Mirror*.

Full court ruling *Attorney General v Associated Newspapers Ltd & Anor* [2011] EWHC 1894 (Admin) (19 July 2011)
http://www.bailii.org/ew/cases/EWHC/Admin/2011/1894.html

This case demonstrates that the crime of media contempt involves publications that create a substantial risk of impeding as well as prejudicing the administration of justice. Impeding justice means disrupting or frustrating a criminal enquiry or preparation of a defence case. Media contempt is not just a matter of prejudicing the minds of jurors.

✪ A downloadable sound file of this section on media contempt committed when demonizing an arrested suspect.
   1.4 podcast downloadable https://soundcloud.com/
   comparativemedialaw/podcast1-4-uk-media-law

1.5 SUCCESSFUL PROSECUTION OF NEWSPAPERS WHO PUBLISHED PREJUDICIAL ONLINE IMAGES OF A DEFENDANT

On 3 March 2011 Lord Justice Moses and Mr Justice Owen ruled that the *Daily Mail* and *The Sun* newspapers had created a substantial risk of serious prejudice by publishing online photographs of a defendant, Ryan Ward, when he was on trial at Sheffield Crown Court for murdering a 39-year-old father who had intervened after Ward had head-butted a young woman.

The photograph, taken from a social networking site, depicted Ward holding a pistol. This was the first case of national newspapers in Britain being prosecuted for media contempt by online publication. The jury had been warned not to consult the Internet. After the prosecution opening, the *Mail* online published an image that 'showed Ward holding a pistol in his right hand with his index finger on the trigger whilst he indicated firing a handgun with his left hand'. It remained online for nearly five hours until the mistake had been spotted. Digital data analysis indicated that 112 users in the Sheffield area obtained access to the article. Publication in *The Sun* occurred on the second day of the trial for about 19 hours and 'although the picture was carefully cropped for newspaper publication so as to exclude Ward's left hand and any view of the gun, when the picture was cropped for publication online, the top part, the barrel, of the gun was visible'.

Seventy-eight unique visitors to the article in Sheffield were established. The trial judge established that no members of the jury had seen the online articles. But the Divisional Court ruled 'The criminal courts have been troubled by the dangers to the integrity and fairness of a criminal trial, where juries can obtain such easy access to the internet and to other forms of instant communication. Once information is published on the internet, it is difficult if not impossible completely to remove it.'

The judges concluded: 'we are sure that there was a substantial risk that a juror would see the photograph and that there was a substantial risk of serious prejudice, namely that the jury would have had to be discharged, had that occurred'. Both newspapers were fined £15,000 each and ordered to pay legal costs of just over £28,000.

> Full court ruling *Attorney General v Associated Newspapers Ltd & Anor* [2011] EWHC 418 (Admin) (03 March 2011)
> http://www.bailii.org/ew/cases/EWHC/Admin/2011/418.html

✱   A downloadable sound file on this section concerning media contempt by online image.
1.5 podcast downloadable https://soundcloud.com/comparativemedialaw/podcast1-5-uk-media-law

1.6 SUCCESSFUL PROSECUTION OF THE *SPECTATOR* MAGAZINE FOR COMMENT ARTICLE THAT PREJUDICED OLD BAILEY TRIAL OF TWO MEN LATER CONVICTED OF MURDERING STEPHEN LAWRENCE

On 17 November 2011 the columnist Rod Liddle had written and published an article in the weekly periodical the *Spectator* that coincided with key evidence from a prosecution witness at the Old Bailey trial of two men accused of murdering Stephen Lawrence in 1993. The article stated: 'it would be a singularly perverse judge who took action against me: for the last 18 years the public has been assured that all five of the men originally named as suspects, including Dobson and Norris, were absolutely guilty, bang to rights […] Should we care about these undoubtedly violent, often criminal, certainly unpleasant white trash? That they were (and probably still are) racists is quite beyond dispute.' The article discussed the connections between the five suspects and organized crime as well as the previous convictions of the defendant Norris. Senior District Judge Howard Riddle fined the magazine £3,000 (maximum penalty was £5,000) and ordered it to pay £2,000 compensation to the parents of Stephen Lawrence as well as £610 costs and a £15 victim surcharge. The article was a breach of an order made by the Court of Appeal in September 2010, widely circulated to news organizations, that reporting details of previous convictions and associations of the two accused was postponed until the end of the trial. Breaches of such orders are summarily prosecuted in the lower magistrates' court. The magazine could have been prosecuted for breaching the 1981 Contempt of Court Act at the Divisional Court, but the Attorney General decided to refer the matter to the DPP and CPS for summary jurisdiction and the magazine pleaded guilty and apologized. Judge Riddle said:

> Apart from the fact that the article breached a court order the reality is that as a result of publication there was at least a brief period during a sensitive part of the trial in which the whole trial process itself was in jeopardy. I don't need any imagination whatsoever to see what distress this might have caused, not least to the Lawrence family and friends. Fortunately it is clear that the jury did not read the article and the trial was able to come to a fair conclusion. But for Mr and Mrs Lawrence and members of their family the prospect of the trial collapsing must have been terrifying.

CPS announcement of charge
http://www.cps.gov.uk/news/press_statements/charging_
announcement_regarding_the_spectator_magazine/index.html
Report by PA Media Lawyer in *Press Gazette* of guilty plea and sentence
17 June 2012
http://www.pressgazette.co.uk/story.asp?storycode=49452
Sections 82 and 83 of the Criminal Justice Act 2003
http://www.legislation.gov.uk/ukpga/2003/44/part/10/enacted

✻   A downloadable sound file on media contempt by publishing
    a seriously prejudicial article after a trial has started.
    1.6 podcast downloadable https://soundcloud.com/
    comparativemedialaw/podcast1-6-uk-media-law

1.7 PROSECUTION OF TWO NATIONAL NEWSPAPERS FOR PUBLISHING BACKGROUND IN TRIAL OF SERIAL KILLER WHO MURDERED MILLY DOWLER WHEN JURORS WERE STILL DECIDING ON A LESSER CHARGE FOR AN ATTEMPTED KIDNAP OFFENCE IN RELATION TO ANOTHER VICTIM

In May 2011 Levi Bellfield was tried for the murder of 13-year-old Milly Dowler on 21 March 2002 and the attempted kidnap of 11-year-old Rachel Cowles on the previous day. The jury knew he had been convicted on 25 February 2008 of murdering Marsha McDonnell on 4 February 2003, Amelie Delagrange on 19 August 2004, and the attempted murder of Kate Sheedy on 28 May 2004. The jury found him guilty of kidnapping and murdering Milly Dowler on 23 June 2011 and while they continued their deliberations, the broadcast media and national newspapers published background about Bellfield not part of the evidence at the trial and despite an email warning from the CPS that nothing should be published that might prejudice the jury in its ongoing deliberations. The Attorney General prosecuted two national newspapers for contempt and the President of the Queen's Bench Division ruled they were guilty because: 'the articles in the *Daily Mail* purported to link Bellfield to another murder and more importantly put forward an account of the drug induced rape of schoolgirls. The article in the *Daily Mirror* set out his rape of a disabled girl on a car bonnet and his depraved sexual abuse of two of the witnesses who had not given evidence of these matters.' The articles were highly prejudicial because they 'set out material in relation to his sexual perversion in relation to his partners and his perverted interest in and rape of girls'. The newspapers had argued that: 'Given what the jury knew about the depravity of Bellfield, these further descriptions of his depravity could not have resulted in a substantial risk of serious prejudice to the proceedings. [...] There was nothing in the material published which was directly relevant to the count of attempted kidnapping that the jury was considering.' The newspapers argued that TV news channels such as Sky, ITN and the BBC had broadcast background not known to the jury, but the court ruled: 'none carried the allegations of a sexual interest in girls or his rape of girls'.

Full court ruling HM *Attorney General v Associated Newspapers Ltd & Anor* [2012] EWHC 2029 (Admin) (18 July 2012)
http://www.bailii.org/ew/cases/EWHC/Admin/2012/2029.html
Newspapers each fined £10,000 for contempt with £25,000 legal costs in trial of Levi Bellfield:
Attorney General v Associated Newspapers Ltd & Anor [2012] EWHC B19 (QB) (16 October 2012)
http://www.bailii.org/ew/cases/EWHC/QB/2012/B19.html

✴   A downloadable sound file of this section on media contempt by publication while a jury is still considering verdicts.
1.7 podcast downloadable https://soundcloud.com/comparativemedialaw/podcast1-7-uk-media-law

1.8   SUCCESSFUL PROSECUTIONS OF JUROR WHO CARRIED OUT INTERNET RESEARCH AND USED FACEBOOK TO CONTACT AN ACQUITTED DEFENDANT

The Attorney General has successfully pursued two prosecutions against jurors who defied trial judge directions not to consult the Internet and/or social media to communicate and obtain information. On 16 June 2011 the Lord Chief Justice ruled that juror Joanne Fraill had committed contempt of court when she communicated with an acquitted defendant, Jamie Sewart, on the social networking site Facebook during a trial at Manchester Crown Court that had been the third attempt to prosecute the accused.

Fraill had the following text message exchange with Sewart: 'cant get anywaone to go either no one budging pleeeeeese don't say anything cause jamie they could call mmisstrial and I will get 4cked toO'. This led to the response from Sewart 'I know I have deleted all the messages'. The court declared: 'the confidentiality required of jurors throughout the trial continues indefinitely after its conclusion … Misuse of the internet by a juror, or contravention of the contempt of court provisions in section 8(1) of the 1981 Act is always a most serious irregularity and contempt.'

Her contemptuous behaviour meant a new trial was ordered on the counts where verdicts were awaited. There had also been evidence in her diary that she had carried out Internet research on the names of people who featured in the trial. Fraill was jailed for eight months. Sewart received a two-month prison sentence suspended for two years.

Full court ruling *Attorney General v Fraill & Ors* [2011] EWCH 1629 (Admin) (16 June 2011)
http://www.bailii.org/ew/cases/EWHC/Admin/2011/1629.html

★   A downloadable sound file of this section on media contempt by a juror in defiance of a judge's direction.
1.8 podcast downloadable https://soundcloud.com/comparativemedialaw/podcast1-8-uk-media-law

1.9   SUCCESSFUL PROSECUTION OF JUROR WHO CARRIED OUT INTERNET RESEARCH ABOUT DEFENDANT'S BACKGROUND AND TOLD THE OTHER JURORS DURING THEIR DELIBERATIONS

On 23 January 2012 the Lord Chief Justice jailed a university psychology lecturer, Dr Theodora Dallas, for six months for carrying out online research about a man on trial at Luton Crown Court accused of causing grievous bodily harm. She had learned that he had been previously acquitted of rape and told her fellow jurors about what she had discovered. The trial was aborted after her conduct was reported to the judge.

Dr Dallas explained that she had carried out the research because she had been having language difficulties and apologized, but Lord Judge said: 'The damage to the administration of justice is obvious. Misuse of the Internet by a juror is always a most serious irregularity and an effective custodial sentence is virtually inevitable.'

Attorney General's statement on sentencing of Dr Dallas
http://www.attorneygeneral.gov.uk/NewsCentre/Pages/
Jurorconvictedforinternetsearches.aspx

✳   A downloadable sound file of this summary of media contempt by a juror carrying out Internet research on a case she was trying.
1.9 podcast downloadable https://soundcloud.com/comparativemedialaw/podcast1-9-uk-media-law

1.10 ATTORNEY GENERAL V FIVE NATIONAL NEWSPAPERS OVER PREJUDICIAL REPORTING OF THE CASE OF MICHAEL FAGAN WHO WALKED INTO THE QUEEN'S BEDROOM

The first test case for media contempt was the prosecution of five national newspapers over their coverage of the case of Michael Fagan after he had been arrested and charged for burglary following his uninvited visit to the Queen's bedroom in 1982. Apartments surrounding Buckingham Palace provide homes for serving staff and loyal retainers. Palace security, though tight, has been breached on a number of occasions. In 1840, 17-year-old Edmund Jones was found underneath a sofa on which Queen Victoria had been sitting moments earlier. He had entered through an open window out of curiosity.

On the morning of 9 July 1982, 35-year-old Michael Fagan shinned up a drainpipe and entered the Queen's bedroom. The

Queen's account of what happened was not revealed in open court at Mr Fagan's trial. In 2012 he described the incident in an interview with the *Independent* newspaper and explained that the Queen left her bedroom to summon help as soon as he appeared before her.

'Michael Fagan: "Her nightie was one of those Liberty prints, down to her knees"'
http://www.independent.co.uk/news/people/profiles/michael-fagan-her-nightie-was-one-of-those-liberty-prints-down-to-her-knees-7179547.html

The five newspapers were prosecuted under the new 1981 Contempt of Court Act for creating a substantial risk of serious prejudice to Mr Fagan's trial for burglary at Buckingham Palace, assaulting his stepson and taking his common law wife's car without her consent. The sensational nature of the case hinged on the fact that security was so bad at the Palace that Fagan had managed to climb through a window on two different occasions. During his first visit he had helped himself to half a bottle of sweet white wine, a wedding present to Prince Charles and Diana Spencer, but had not had enough courage to knock on the Queen's door. The following week, he plucked up enough courage and simply walked into the Queen's bedroom while she was in bed waiting for her morning tea.

Three of these publications were cleared of contempt because the prejudicial comment was not judged to go to the heart of the issues to be decided later at the trial. Furthermore the judges did not think potential members of the jury would remember these observations. This was the first test of what was considered to be 'serious prejudice' and a 'substantial risk'. Convictions were brought against two newspapers, which had falsely reported that Michael Fagan 'had confessed to burglary' and that he had 'stabbed his stepson with a screwdriver'. The actual allegation only concerned 'slapping'.

The Sun made Fagan out to have a long-standing drug problem (asserting he was a 'junkie'), that he was a glib liar and that he had stolen cigars from the Palace. In alleged interviews with his parents it was stated that Fagan was good with locks, 'was a real Spider-man and jumped over walls as though they were not there' and his father was quoted as saying 'he'd been smoking expensive cigars recently and we wondered if they were Prince Philip's'. The Lord Chief Justice at the time, Lord Geoffrey Lane, ruled that this was not contempt as it was thought that the risk of prejudice that the article created was too remote to qualify as 'substantial'.

The *Sunday People* described Fagan as 'a morose, unsociable, unpredictable misfit'. It said he was a heroin addict and used the term 'junkie'. Lord Lane said the allegations were similar to those made by *The Sun* and did not amount to a substantial risk of serious prejudice.

The *Daily Star* asserted that Fagan had admitted stealing the wine. This was held to be in contempt. Lord Lane said such an allegation, which was not true, created 'a very substantial risk of serious prejudice'.

The *Mail on Sunday* contained a clear suggestion of a possible homosexual liaison between Commander Trestrail (the then royal bodyguard) and Fagan. It also referred to Fagan as a 'rootless neurotic with no visible means of support'. Lord Lane said this created a substantial risk of serious prejudice: 'A suggestion of the rootless penniless neurotic being a guest of the homosexual royal bodyguard at the Palace created a picture which tended to stay in the mind and was not easy to dismiss.' However the newspaper was acquitted because they had a defence under section 5 of the Act. The editorial column by Lady Marcia Falkender had been a discussion of the Queen's security, in the public interest, and was 'merely incidental to court proceedings' against Michael Fagan.

The *Sunday Times* had published two articles. The first prominently published on the front page the allegation that Fagan was charged with stabbing his stepson in the neck. Lord Lane said this was contempt because he had been charged with assault and not stabbing. This gross misrepresentation did create a substantial risk of serious prejudice. The second article suggested that the driving charge had been dropped and that the stepson's injuries had been received in some earlier incident before Fagan arrived. This was held to be contempt on the grounds it was prejudicial to the prosecution's case. The *Sunday Times* was fined £1,000. No penalty was made against the *Daily Star*.

✱   A downloadable sound file of this section on the first prosecution for media contempt under the 1981 Contempt of Court Act over press coverage of the Queen's bedroom intruder.
1.10 podcast downloadable https://soundcloud.com/comparativemedialaw/podcast1-10-uk-media-law

1.11   USE OF TWITTER AND LAPTOP WI-FI/EMAIL IN COURT REPORTING, PROHIBITION ON PHOTOGRAPHY AND UNAUTHORIZED USE OF SOUND RECORDING

The Lord Chief Justice of England and Wales, Lord Igor Judge, issued a guidance notice effective from 14 December 2011. There is no requirement for journalists and legal commentators to seek permission to use text-based devices to communicate from court. These include hand-held computer devices such as a BlackBerry or iPhone and laptop/notebook computers with Wi-Fi/mobile radio communications. Members of the public will have to apply, formally or informally, if they want to do so: 'The use of live text-based forms of communication (including Twitter) from court for the purposes of fair and accurate reporting' relates to court proceedings which are open to the public and 'to those parts of the proceedings which are not subject to reporting restrictions'.

Photography in court remains strictly forbidden as there is a statutory prohibition under the 1925 Administration of Justice Act. Sound recordings may only be made with the court's consent and will only be for note-taking purposes and not for broadcasting as set out in section 9 of the 1981 Contempt of Court Act and subsequent Practice Directions.

The guidance cautions about the use of such devices during hearings about inadmissible evidence that 'may influence members of a jury', and the risk that 'witnesses who are out of court may be informed of what has already happened in court and so coached or briefed before they give evidence'. Electronic texting has to comply with reporting restrictions as in the case of any previous method of reporting. Judges are warned to be mindful of how simultaneous reporting from the courtroom could put pressure on witnesses, particularly in family and civil proceedings.

For practical purposes, professional journalists should have verifiable identification (e.g. a CIoJ or NUJ ACPO approved card) and identify their status and presence to court staff beforehand and also indicate to the clerk of the court that they intend to electronically report from the courtroom. Having a copy of the Lord Chief Justice's guidance would also be helpful. Any method of disabling the photographic, video and sound recording function of the electronic machines used would be helpful and if this were not possible, journalists would have to take very special care that none of these prohibitive functions were activated accidentally.

A key quotation from the guidance states: 'the use of an unobtrusive, hand held, silent piece of modern equipment for the purposes of simultaneous reporting of proceedings to the outside world as they unfold in court is generally unlikely to interfere with the proper administration of justice'. The key words are clearly 'unobtrusive' and 'silent'.

Lord Chief Justice's 'Practice Guidance' on tweeting and live text-based communication
http://www.judiciary.gov.uk/Resources/JCO/Documents/Guidance/ltbc-guidance-dec–2011.pdf

---

✶   A downloadable sound file of this section on tweeting from court.
1.11 podcast downloadable https://soundcloud.com/comparativemedialaw/podcast1-11-uk-media-law

1.12 POSTPONING REPORTS OF TRIALS TO AVOID PREJUDICE

Courts have the power to order the postponement of information, parts of trials and whole trials under section 4(2) of the 1981 Contempt of Court Act in order to avoid prejudice to the administration of justice. Such orders need to state clearly what the media is postponed from reporting (extent) and the exact time when the order ceases to apply (usually return of all verdicts). Section 4(1) of the 1981 Contempt of Court Act states that no person can be guilty of contempt for publishing fair, accurate and contemporaneous reports of court proceedings in good faith where no orders have been made.

These orders are usually issued to cover parts of jury trials heard in the absence of the jury where arguments about inadmissible evidence are ventilated. The freedom of expression Article 10 of the HRA places a legal obligation on courts to minimize the derogation from the open justice principle. The orders can also be made in relation to the ordering of retrials following successful appeals against conviction, an overriding of the double jeopardy rule when new evidence has emerged to justify the Appeal Court permitting a fresh prosecution of a case previously ending in acquittal, and where a previous trial was deemed to have been corrupted by intimidation or bribery of the jurors. Sometimes a complicated case can be prosecuted by a series of trials connected to the same crime and the trial judge has decided that contemporaneous reporting of trial 1 will prejudice trials 2 or 3 and a section 4(2) Order will apply until the conclusion (return of all verdicts) in the last trial of the series.

B, Re [2006] EWCA Crim 2692 (27 October 2006)
http://www.bailii.org/ew/cases/EWCA/Crim/2006/2692.html
R v Sherwood ex parte Telegraph Group and ors [2001] EWCA Crim 1075
(3 May 2001)
http://www.bailii.org/ew/cases/EWCA/Crim/2001/1075.html
Times Newspapers Ltd & Others v R on appeal from the Central
Criminal Court [2007] EWCA Crim 1925 (30 July 2007)
http://www.bailii.org/ew/cases/EWCA/Crim/2007/1925.html

✷   A downloadable sound file of this section on the power of UK
      judges to postpone reporting of trial proceedings.
      1.12 podcast downloadable https://soundcloud.com/
      comparativemedialaw/podcast1-12-uk-media-law

1.13 PROHIBITING PUBLICATION OF MATTERS WITHHELD FROM THE PUBLIC BEFORE PROCEEDINGS

Courts have the power to prohibit media publication of matters
withheld from the public before the proceedings under section 11
of the 1981 Contempt of Court Act. This relates to anonymous
witnesses who fear reprisals or complainants of blackmail where
the threatened menaces are embarrassing. The orders should only
be used where the courts had a previous common law power to
conceal the information.

These orders are occasionally made in relation to information
revealed to the public in open court and this is strictly not empow-
ered by the legislation. Orders that prohibit media reporting should
be constructed from the legislation providing the power to do so.

Trinity Mirror & Ors, R (on the application of) v Croydon Crown Court
[2008] EWCA Crim 50 (01 February 2008)
http://www.bailii.org/ew/cases/EWCA/Crim/2008/50.html

✷   A downloadable sound file on section 11 orders banning
      publication of information withheld from open court.
      1.13 podcast downloadable https://soundcloud.com/
      comparativemedialaw/podcast1-13-uk-media-law

1.14 TELEVISION AND RADIO COVERAGE OF THE COURTS

The 1925 Administration of Justice Act prohibits the use of
cameras or live sketching during court proceedings in England
and Wales. The legislation does not apply in Scotland. Scottish

judges therefore have discretion to permit photography, filming or sketching. It is also an offence to photograph and film people entering and leaving 'court precincts'. It would be advisable to find out what constitutes the precincts at specific court complexes so that camera/tripod positions are not challenged by the police.

Section 9 of the 1981 Contempt of Court Act makes it an offence to use a tape recorder or bring into a court a tape recorder for use without leave of the court. There are also Practice Directions from the Lord Chief Justice of England and Wales prohibiting the broadcasting of tape recordings of court hearings. However, unlike cameras, in theory reporters should be able to use devices to record sound interviews in a court building outside the courtrooms. Security personnel are usually instructed to prohibit media personnel bringing into court buildings camera or sound recording equipment. It is useful to make arrangements with nearby shops and commercial premises to leave the machinery to be picked up after the hearing and it is not unknown for the proprietors to do this in return for a modest fee of 50p or £1.

The Scottish legal system has permitted broadcasting of criminal proceedings, though with very restrictive qualifications and permission arrangements. In May 2012 the UK government supported legislative reform allowing broadcasting of court proceedings in England and Wales through the Crime and Courts Bill. Clause 22 essentially gives the Lord Chancellor (also Secretary of State for Justice), with the agreement of the Lord Chief Justice of England and Wales, the power to override the prohibition on pictures and sound in section 41 of the Criminal Justice Act 1925 and section 9 of the Contempt of Court Act 1981. Courts and tribunals will have the power to deny televising or sound broadcasting in order to 'ensure the fairness of any particular proceedings [...] or to ensure that any person involved in the proceedings is not unduly prejudiced'. No appeal will be allowed against any such decision and it has been made clear that broadcasting will be restricted to lawyers making opening and closing speeches, and judges' decisions and sentencing; witnesses, jurors and defendants will remain out of view.

Clause 22 of the Crime and Courts Bill 2012
http://www.publications.parliament.uk/pa/bills/lbill/2012–2013/0004/
lbill_2012–20130004_en_4.htm#pt2-pb1-l1g22

★   A downloadable sound file of this section on restrictions and
rights in respect of sound and visual reporting of UK courts.
1.14 podcast downloadable https://soundcloud.com/
comparativemedialaw/podcast1-14-uk-media-law

1.15 PROTECTING AND REPORTING THE VIEWS OF JURORS

Section 8 of the 1981 Contempt of Court Act makes it an offence
for jurors to communicate information about their deliberations on
the verdict(s) or for journalists to solicit jurors about their deliberations. The contempt offence should not prevent jurors being interviewed about their experiences outside the deliberation process
or for their opinions about many aspects of the trial such as the
judge, conduct of lawyers, and outcome of the case such as verdict
and/or sentence. However, the judiciary is very sensitive to media
approaches to and dialogue with jurors.

There is a tendency for judges to create a *cordon sanitaire* around
jurors in terms of their identity. Sketching, photographing and
filming of jurors could be considered 'impeding' the administration
of justice. This is despite the fact that jurors answer to their names
when sworn in and are rarely concealed in public proceedings. It
would not be advisable to report/publish the names of jurors and it
might well be considered a contempt of court to do so. There have
been occasions when jurors have discussed their concerns that jury
decisions could amount to a miscarriage of justice. The ECtHR
case in 2012 involving an appeal by a jury foreman and *The Times*
newspaper over a conviction for contempt by revealing jury deliberation suggests that Article 10 freedom of expression rights do not
trump existing UK legislative law on this issue.

Michael Alexander Seckerson & Times Newspapers Ltd v the United Kingdom App Nos 32844/10 and 33510/10 [2012] ECtHR 241 (24 January 2012)
http://www.bailii.org/eu/cases/ECHR/2012/241.htm

✳ Downloadable sound file on reporting media contempt in relation to reporting jurors' views and interviewing them about proceedings.
1.15 podcast downloadable https://soundcloud.com/comparativemedialaw/podcast1-15-uk-media-law

1.16 KEY RESTRICTIONS APPLYING TO NEWSWORTHY FIRST COURT APPEARANCES AT MAGISTRATES' COURTS

Under section 8 of the Magistrates' Court Act 1980 first court hearings of very serious cases (to be tried at Crown Court) are subject to restrictions. These hearings are sometimes known as 'committal proceedings'. The reporting restrictions can be lifted but this has to be by application and permission of all defendant(s).

These restrictions apply only to court proceedings (not what happens outside court). What happens outside court is subject to the strict liability rule: substantial risk of serious prejudice/impeding justice, and libel.

The ten-points rule technically has no leeway but it is not uncommon for media journalists to report minor details which are neither prejudicial nor issues in the later trial. How the accused persons are dressed is often reported even though it might be a technical breach of the restrictions. Saying the public gallery was packed and that a girlfriend or wife waved and smiled at the defendant in the dock is unlikely to attract a prosecution.

The ten points are:

1   name of the court
2   names of magistrate or examining justices
3   names, ages, addresses, occupations of parties, defendants/witnesses

4   the charge or charges
5   the names of counsel (barristers or QCs) and solicitors
6   the decision to commit or how the case was disposed of
7   the charges on which each defendant was committed
8   the date and place to which the hearing was adjourned or the case committed
9   arrangements for bail and whether bail was granted
10 whether legal aid was granted or refused.

In 1973 the *Eastbourne Herald* was unfairly prosecuted and fined £200 for including in a remand hearing report that the defendant was a 'New Year's Day Bridegroom ... bespectacled and dark-suited' and the charges were 'serious'. Geoffrey Robertson and Andrew Nicol in their textbook *Media Law* have rightly pointed out that an appeal would have been successful because these matters were 'not part of the proceedings'. It is important to remember that the restrictions permit reporting arrangements for bail, but whether it is granted or not, it would be a breach to report any reasons argued for or against such as police fears of absconding, committing further offences or intimidating witnesses.

★   Downloadable sound file on reporting first magistrates' court appearance in cases going to crown court for trial.
    1.16 podcast downloadable https://soundcloud.com/comparativemedialaw/podcast1-16-uk-media-law

1.17 OTHER AUTOMATIC AND DISCRETIONARY RESTRICTIONS AFFECTING REPORTING

Depending on the depth and sophistication of your reporting, writing and communicating about the British legal system you need to be aware of restrictions applying to specialist hearings and unusual situations:

a   Pre-trial hearings where rulings are made on admissibility of evidence. Restrictions usually apply until the trial has been concluded.

> See section 41 of the Criminal Procedure and Investigations Act
> 1996: http://www.legislation.gov.uk/ukpga/1996/25/section/41

b   There are also restrictions imposed in what are known as 'preparatory hearings' at the Crown Court where the judge, prosecution and defence discuss the management and direction of the future trials of long, complex or serious cases.

> See section 37 of the Criminal Procedure and Investigations Act
> 1996: http://www.legislation.gov.uk/ukpga/1996/25/section/37
> and section 11 of the Criminal Justice Act 1987: http://www.
> legislation.gov.uk/ukpga/1987/38/section/11

c   Unsuccessful dismissal of proceedings when application is made by persons accused of fraud, sexual offences or cruelty against children.

> See section 11 Criminal Justice Act 1987: http://www.legislation.
> gov.uk/ukpga/1987/38/section/11; section 53, Schedule 6,
> paragraph 6 Criminal Justice Act 1991: http://www.legislation.
> gov.uk/ukpga/1991/53/schedule/6; and Schedule 3, paragraph 3
> of Crime and Disorder Act 1998: http://www.legislation.gov.uk/
> ukpga/1998/37/schedule/3

d   Special measures and directions for the protection of witnesses. These relate to protections and special measures for witnesses using live video link, pseudonym identities, and preventing the accused from cross-examining a witness in person.

> See section 47 of the Youth Justice and Criminal Evidence Act
> 1999: http://www.legislation.gov.uk/ukpga/1999/23/section/47

e   Prohibition of detail that is indecent, medical, surgical or physiological that is 'calculated to injure public morals'.

> See section 1 of the Judicial Proceedings (Regulation of Reports) Act
> 1926: http://www.legislation.gov.uk/ukpga/Geo5/16–17/61/section/1

f   Postponement of derogatory remarks made in mitigation. Courts can postpone reports of 'derogatory assertions' made about named or identified persons in a mitigation speech by defence lawyers during a sentencing hearing. The order should not be made if the allegation had been made during open trial and previous proceedings, and the order lasts for a period of 12 months.

> See section 58 of the Criminal Procedure and Investigations Act 1996: http://www.legislation.gov.uk/ukpga/1996/25/section/58

g   Automatic reporting restrictions apply when the prosecution informs the court of its intention to appeal against the court's rulings and to the court's subsequent decision as to whether to expedite the prosecution appeal, or adjourn, or discharge the jury. All these legal matters take place in the absence of the jury so it should be obvious to any trained and experienced journalist that these matters should not be published.

> See section 71 of the Criminal Justice Act 2003:
> http://www.legislation.gov.uk/ukpga/2003/44/section/71

h   In October 2012 statutory anonymity for teachers accused of crime against children in their care until formally charged under section 13 of the 2011 Education Act came into force and the Leveson Inquiry Report recommended legal legitimizing of anonymity for all suspects at the time of their arrest until charged.

> Reporting restrictions on reporting alleged offences by teachers
> http://www.legislation.gov.uk/ukpga/2011/21/section/13/enacted

The new restriction is complicated and contains qualifications where a teacher waives anonymity, or is named by the Secretary of State for Education as being subject to disciplinary action.

The respected media law trainer Cleland Thom has analysed the complexity of the restriction.

> Loopholes for journalists in the new teacher anonymity law: What you can safely report
> http://www.pressgazette.co.uk/content/
> loopholes-journalists-new-teacher-anonymity-law

Lord Justice Leveson advocated in his inquiry report in November 2012 that all suspects arrested should not be identified by police to the media either on the record or off the record until charged, thus triggering the difficulties that media organizations have in relation to libel and applying the strict liability rule of the 1981 Contempt of Court Act, which applies when a case is active from the time of arrest.

The breach of these reporting restrictions attracts different levels of prosecution compared to media contempt of court (usually summary prosecution at magistrates' court and a fine/non-custodial penalty).

★   Downloadable sound file on section covering other reporting restrictions in the criminal courts.
    1.17 podcast downloadable https://soundcloud.com/
    comparativemedialaw/podcast1-17-uk-media-law

1.18 BREACHING COURT INJUNCTIONS AND DIRECTIONS

If any court makes an order postponing or prohibiting publication in any form, it could be a contempt of court to intentionally or unintentionally subvert it, breach it or defy it. You can be in contempt of court 'by accident' if it can be shown that you acted in bad faith throughout. Even if you believe that the court has made a wrong order in law, this does not give you any justification to breach the court order.

If you are aware that the information you are banned from publishing is being published online, by others inside or outside the legal jurisdiction of England and Wales, Scotland, or Northern Ireland, copying and publishing the information gives you no defence. If a court order is made in only the English (and Welsh) jurisdiction and no attempt has been made to apply for an equivalent order in the Scottish jurisdiction (which has a separate legal system independent of England and Wales) then the English court order will not apply in Scotland and it may be the case that the Scottish media will be disseminating information banned in England and Wales.

While Westminster parliamentarians have freedom of speech immunity against court orders under the 1689 Bill of Rights it is arguable that this does not extend to the media and people who wish to report the breaching of injunctions/court orders by MPs or peers (members of the House of Lords). The nature of the platform for communicating a breach of a court order makes no difference to the construction of the offence, though may be mitigation in terms of the sentence. Hence, the use of Twitter, the Internet, social networking, pamphlets, speaking in public, person-to-person verbal contact and email is treated the same as radio, television, newspaper, magazine or book publication. Bloggers, 'citizen journalists', tweeters and non-journalists are treated in the same way as accredited media professionals. When criminal offences are being investigated and the liberty of people is at issue in criminal enquiries, courts in foreign jurisdictions can be persuaded to order Internet, digital mobile media, and social networking platforms, based overseas, to hand over the content of potentially contemptuous communications and reveal the full identity of the authors.

✶ Downloadable sound file of this section explaining the consequences of breaching court orders.
1.18 podcast downloadable https://soundcloud.com/comparativemedialaw/podcast1-18-uk-media-law

1.19 DEFENCES AND CHALLENGES

In the United Kingdom there is a well-established common law 'open justice' principle that is reinforced by Article 10 of the HRA, derived from Article 10 of the ECHR:

Article 10 Freedom of expression:

1   Everyone has the right to freedom of expression. This right shall include freedom to hold opinions and to receive and impart information and ideas without interference by public authority and regardless of frontiers. This Article shall not prevent States from requiring the licensing of broadcasting, television or cinema enterprises.

2   The exercise of these freedoms, since it carries with it duties and responsibilities, may be subject to such formalities, conditions, restrictions or penalties as are prescribed by law and are necessary in a democratic society, in the interests of national security, territorial integrity or public safety, for the prevention of disorder or crime, for the protection of health or morals, for the protection of the reputation or rights of others, for preventing the disclosure of information received in confidence, or for maintaining the authority and impartiality of the judiciary.

---

http://www.legislation.gov.uk/ukpga/1998/42/schedule/1

Furthermore, the legislation, under section 12, does give freedom of expression an emphasis, if not priority, when a balance needs to be considered by the courts in relation to other Convention rights:

3   The court must have particular regard to the importance of the Convention right to freedom of expression and, where the proceedings relate to material which the respondent claims, or which appears to the court, to be journalistic, literary or artistic material (or to conduct connected with such material), to—

a   the extent to which—

- i   the material has, or is about to, become available to the public; or
- ii   it is, or would be, in the public interest for the material to be published;

b   any relevant privacy code.

---

http://www.legislation.gov.uk/ukpga/1998/42/section/12

Whilst this book focuses on what journalists and media communicators should not do, it is important to appreciate that media law controls have to be balanced with a common law principle of freedom of expression developed over centuries of history, and Article 10 of the Human Rights Act 1998 derived from the ECHR. The Leveson Inquiry Report of 2012 advocated that legislation be passed defining a constitutional freedom of the media:

Guarantee of Media Freedom:

1   The Secretary of State for Culture, Media and Sport and other Ministers of the Crown and all with responsibility for matters relating to the media must uphold the freedom of the press and its independence from the executive;

2   The Secretary of State for Culture, Media and Sport must have regard to:

a   the importance of the freedom and integrity of the media;

b   the right of the media and the public to receive and impart information without interference by public authorities;

c   the need to defend the independence of the media;

3   Interference with the activities of the media shall be lawful only insofar as it is for a legitimate purpose and is necessary in a democratic society, having full regard to the importance of media freedom in a democracy. (page 1780, Volume 4, *An Inquiry into the Culture, Practices and Ethics of the Press*, HMSO 2012)

It is possible that this rubric will be referenced in future litigation and case law.

Open justice means that court proceedings (the administration of justice) should be done in public, with the public and media having a right to attend, and enabled to report fully and contemporaneously. Restrictions imposed by court order, whether statutory or discretionary, should be exceptional, and necessary in terms of proportionality, with a pressing social need in the context of a democratic society. This means that statutory postponement and prohibition (whether declared by Act of Parliament or statutory instrument such as Practice Directions) could be incompatible with the ECHR.

Section 16 of the Criminal Procedure Rules 2011 No. 1709 (L. 15):

a   directs all courts to have regard to the importance of dealing with criminal cases in public and allowing them to be reported;
b   imposes a duty on courts to ensure that all the parties involved and 'any other person directly affected' i.e. the press and media is either present or has had an opportunity to attend or make representations before reporting restrictions are imposed.

See section 16 of Criminal Procedure Rules 2011
http://www.legislation.gov.uk/uksi/2011/1709/part/16/made

As an accredited and assigned journalist, or legitimate journalistic publisher, you could find yourself in three positions when attending court as a media communicator: reporter, person subject to reporting restriction, person accused of breaching a reporting restriction/contempt of court. As a reporter it is advisable to dress and conduct yourself in a respectful manner to take into account the professional and cultural ritual of court proceedings. The parties are usually under considerable emotional and intellectual pressure. They expect the media to take the process seriously and appreciate the position and feelings of everyone involved in a process of justice. The trial forum is not unlike a religious ritual such as a church, mosque, synagogue or temple service. Making respectful and clear contact with court officers, ushers and officials means that everyone will know who you are and return the respect you offer them.

Should you find yourself in a position to challenge or address the court on a reporting restriction matter it is advisable to have to hand the pdf files of section 16 of the Criminal Procedure Rules 2011 and the guidelines to Reporting Restrictions in the Criminal Courts jointly published by the Judicial Studies Board (JSB), Newspaper Society, Society of Editors and Times Newspapers Ltd in 2009.

'New guidelines issued for reporting restrictions in the criminal courts' http://www.judiciary.gov.uk/media/media-releases/2009/ News-release–2609 Pdf at: http://www.judiciary.gov.uk/Resources/JCO/Documents/ Guidance/crown_court_reporting_restrictions_021009.pdf

You might want to quickly write a note/letter for the judge/court along these lines:

From: name, publisher, telephone number, address, email address

To: His Honour/Mr Justice, etc [it is important to address the judge with the proper title]

Dear Judge Smith/Mrs Justice Smith,
I am a reporter for the XY community news-site published at [URL] and wish to challenge the order you made on [date] in the case of [R v X, Y Z (names of defendants if known)] under section 4(2) of the 1981 Contempt of Court Act.

My argument is based on Article 10 of the Human Rights Act 1998 that the order is not proportionate or necessary in terms of a pressing social need in a democratic society and undermines my right to the freedom of expression to report this case fairly, accurately and contemporaneously.

The copy of the order I have does not indicate when the restriction ends, it prevents me from reporting all of the proceedings, when I believe it should only apply to the legal argument heard in the absence of the jury. When it was made, I understand that no members or representatives of the media were present to address you or guide you in terms of the importance of dealing with criminal cases in public and allowing them to be reported under section 16 of the Criminal Procedure Rules 2011. I believe that the Court of Appeal case of R v Sherwood ex parte The Telegraph Group and ors [2001] EWCA Crim 1075 (3rd May, 2001) online transcript at: http://www.bailii.org/ew/cases/EWCA/Crim/2001/1075.html may assist you in appreciating why I believe you should consider varying or lifting your order.

Should you wish to hear oral submissions on my part, I would be happy to do so either before or at the end of today's proceedings or at another convenient time, though it would be best if the matter was resolved as soon as possible. Equally I am happy for you to consider my application in the form of this letter. I have no wish to disrupt the complicated and demanding task you have of conducting the trial.

It may be the case you have not had immediate access to the Judicial Studies Board guidance on reporting restrictions in the criminal courts (2009) or the detail of the Criminal Procedure Rules 2011 and I am happy to attach these if they should be of assistance.

Yours sincerely and respectfully,
Name/signature.

This pro forma is offered by way of an example. It can be adapted to any of the reporting restriction situations you may find yourself in and can be added to and subtracted from in order to fit any set of circumstances in relation to contempt and issues of anonymity, privacy and media and public exclusion and secrecy orders referred to in Chapters 3, 4 and 8.

The last and obviously least fortunate position you might find yourself in is as a person accused of contempt of court. You must seek immediate legal advice, first by contacting your employing media organization. You should not be dealt with summarily as media contempt issues should by precedent be referred by the courts to the Attorney General for consideration. But if you are summoned to appear to make an explanation, you should have legal representation.

It is advisable not to admit to committing contempt of court, but certainly it helps to be humble, apologetic for any disruption and inconvenience your alleged conduct has caused. An expression of humility combined with the obvious need for you to seek legal advice before explaining or elucidating on the situation is the best holding position. It is advisable that you are a member of a professional journalists' trade union organization such as the Chartered Institute of Journalists or National Union of Journalists, which provide emergency legal advice to members. There are specialist insurers that provide media law protection policies for individual journalists.

There may be a myriad of defences that you are entitled to. These could include mistaken identity in terms of publication (something that can be easily established) or a non-distribution or inadequate dissemination of the court order. Any evidence of the effort you made in good faith to establish the existence of court reporting restrictions in terms of email, notes etc would be helpful. Your reporting may not be proven beyond reasonable doubt to breach the strict liability rule. In common law contempt you may not have had an intention to commit contempt. The court order may have been constructed in its writing in such a way as not to render you in breach of it. In other words the judge may have executed a wrong expression of his/her intention. Should you find yourself in this position, the engagement of specialist legal representation and advice is an absolute necessity.

★   A downloadable sound file voicing this section on potential defences and challenges to media reporting restrictions. 1.19 podcast downloadable https://soundcloud.com/ comparativemedialaw/podcast1-19-uk-media-law

1.20 LIABILITIES, PENALTIES AND PUNISHMENT

It has already been indicated that the offence of media publication contempt of court is indictable to High Court trial with an unlimited fine and maximum jail sentence of two years. The editor of the offending publication is usually the individual who has to take responsibility in terms of punishment, though in 2012 the last time an editor was dispatched to prison was in 1949 when Silvester Bolam, editor of the *Daily Mirror*, received three months for his paper's contempt of court in reporting a murder case. It published the details of an alleged confession to several murders of a man already under police arrest and included a reference to his drinking the blood of his victims. This was the notorious case of 'acid bath' murderer, John Haigh.

The operation of contempt law at that time was different. The 'motion to commit' was not brought by the Attorney General but by the accused himself. The contempt hearing took place before Haigh's trial so the issue of whether the paper's actual publication was contempt in the context of the accused pleading to insanity was not properly explored. The *Mirror*'s lurid article about Haigh's predilection to vampire-like behaviour did not specifically name him. In addition to jailing the editor, the Lord Chief Justice of the time, Lord Goddard, fined the newspaper £10,000 and described the article as a gross contempt that 'violated every principle of justice and fair play which it has been the pride of this country to extend to the worst of criminals'.

Recent rulings have tended to impose fines of £50,000, £18,000 and £15,000 for publications that did not stop trials and where there was no evidence that the prejudicial material had been seen by the jurors. In 2002 an article in the *Sunday Mirror*, which led to the collapse of the first trial of two Leeds United footballers on charges arising out of an assault on an Asian student, attracted a fine of £75,000 and an order to pay costs of £54,160 (*Attorney General v Mirror Group Newspapers Limited* [2002] EWHC 907).

While the English High Court continues to apply 'corporate'-style penalties, it has been known to impose separate contempt penalties on individual reporters. A BBC broadcast journalist has been fined individually £500 for breaching an anonymity order. The British courts also have the option to make 'wasted costs' orders against publications that undermine expensive trials and court hearings. This power has been in force since 2004 and means that any third party who causes proceedings to be aborted by an 'improper, unreasonable or negligent act or omission' can be ordered by a judge or magistrate to pay the prosecution and defence costs.

Section 93 of the Courts Act 2003
http://www.legislation.gov.uk/ukpga/2003/39/section/93

✶   A downloadable sound file of this section on the history and trend of penalties and punishment for media contempt crime. 1.20 podcast downloadable https://soundcloud.com/comparativemedialaw/podcast1-20-uk-media

1.21 GUILT BY ASSOCIATION

It is a potential disciplinary offence not to have any public interest justification for identifying relatives or friends of people convicted or accused of crime without their consent and when not relevant to the story, as well as not paying 'particular regard' to people in potentially vulnerable positions, such as children who may be witnesses, or victims of crime. Tone and proportion should be taken into account. You are expected to check whether relatives and friends consented to identification; were genuinely relevant to the story; it was in the public interest to mention them; the focus is proportionate; and sufficient care has been taken to protect vulnerable children.

The PCC rejected a complaint over identification of the mother and mother-in-law of an England soccer captain after they were cautioned for shoplifting. It also rejected a complaint from a former Health Secretary married to a judge about their son's involvement in a cocaine possession inquiry. Also rejected were complaints from a councillor whose son was arrested for bootlegging, and a Scottish castle owner whose son-in-law had been arrested for allegedly assaulting her daughter who also lived at the castle. However, the PCC upheld complaints from a councillor over prominent coverage of her son's prosecution for drink driving, and the mother of a 12-year-old girl who objected to her daughter's identification as a witness in an attempted kidnapping.

See PCC rulings:
John Terry v *The Sun* (Report 79, 2009)
http://www.pcc.org.uk/news/index.html?article=NTY5Ng
Hewitt v *The Sun* (Report 79, 2009)
http://www.pcc.org.uk/news/index.html?article=NjA3MA
Sihota v *Slough Express* (Report 40, 1997)
http://www.pcc.org.uk/news/index.html?article=MTk2Ng
Gloag v *Perthshire Advertiser* (Report 75, 2007)
http://www.pcc.org.uk/news/index.html?article=NDYxMQ
See also Gloag v *Scottish Sun*
http://www.pcc.org.uk/news/index.html?article=NDYxMA

Lacey v *Eastbourne Gazette* (Report 44, 1998)
http://www.pcc.org.uk/news/index.html?article=MTg2Nw
Hall v *Eastbourne Argus* (Report 59/60, 2002)
http://www.pcc.org.uk/news/index.html?article=MjA3OQ

✳   A downloadable sound file of this section on media
     regulation of unfair publication of names of people associated
     with crimes.
     1.21 podcast downloadable https://soundcloud.com/
     comparativemedialaw/podcast1-21-uk-media-law

1.22 VICTIMS OF SEXUAL ASSAULT

It will be a potential disciplinary issue (as well as criminal
offence) to identify victims of sexual assault or publish material
likely to contribute to such identification unless there is adequate
justification and you are legally able to do so. There is no public
interest defence in primary or secondary media law. The PCC
has strongly cautioned against publications including 'seemingly
innocuous detail' that can lead to identification and insists on
editors applying 'scrupulous construction' of any such stories.
Where a victim waives his or her anonymity it is essential for
this to be confirmed and obtained in writing and great care
taken that in the subsequent interview the rights of others to

anonymity as the victims of sexual assault are not compromised in any way.

Details seemingly insignificant to a third party can immediately lead to identification. The confidentiality is breached if anyone related to or friendly with the complainant can triangulate the link. This has been so when a newspaper reported the victim's age, health record, attack details and location of the offence together, when the report of a rape trial revealed the victim's clothing at the time of the attack and her hobby, and when the publication of the nature of an injury could have identified an under-age victim. The media law trainer Cleland Thom has cautioned about the dangers of including too much detail in court reporting.

'Too many stories provide far too much detail – a simple guide to avoid breaching reporting restrictions'
http://www.pressgazette.co.uk/content/too-many-stories-provide-far-too-much-detail-simple-guide-avoid-breaching-reporting

---

There is a long-standing professional obligation in the UK media to avoid jigsaw identification (also regarded as a legal requirement and potential criminal offence). Very simply this is where the relationship between accused and victim when publicized would identify a sexual offence complainant. All the media, with no exceptions, have to maintain a policy of either identifying the relationship and making anonymous all those involved, or identifying the defendant only (the victim of a sexual offence can never be identified unless by order of the court and waiving of anonymity) and under no circumstances whatsoever publicizing the defendant's relationship with the complainant. Only sexual offence complainants aged 16 and over have the power to waive their own anonymity. For children under this age, it will be a matter for the courts.

See PCC rulings:
A woman v *Macclesfield Express* (Report 74, 2006)
http://www.pcc.org.uk/news/index.html?article=NDIwMw
Thames Valley Police v *London Metro* (Report 59, 2002)
http://www.pcc.org.uk/news/index.html?article=MjA4Mg
A woman v *Clydebank Post* (Report 41, 1998)
http://www.pcc.org.uk/news/index.html?article=MTk5Mg
A woman v *Strathspey & Badenoch Herald* (Report 75, 2007)
http://www.pcc.org.uk/news/index.html?article=NDY1Nw

✱   A downloadable sound file of this section on protecting
     victims of sexual offences from identification and
     embarrassment.
     1.22 podcast downloadable https://soundcloud.com/
     comparativemedialaw/podcast1-22-uk-media-law

1.23 CONTACTING MEMBERS OF THE UK JUDICIARY FOR COMMENT AND INTERVIEW

UK judges are not allowed to make any comment on the cases they
preside over and they cannot discuss their decisions – particularly
sentences in criminal hearings. They are not permitted to analyse
or comment on decisions made in other court cases. This is also
true of lay magistrates and coroners. The PCC had advised in the
past that as there are no circumstances when judges can speak to
the media in these contexts, any journalistic approaches to them or
their families could constitute ethical harassment. It is possible that
members of the judiciary might be prepared to take part in documentary programmes or features about their general role in the
judiciary, or discussion of legal issues that are not specific to any
cases they have been involved in. This would normally require the
permission of the senior judiciary, or indeed the Lord Chancellor,
and is a matter that would normally be negotiated via the Ministry
of Justice press office or senior administrator in the local Court
Service.

⭐   A downloadable sound file of this section on rules relating to media interviewing of the judiciary.

1.23 podcast downloadable https://soundcloud.com/comparativemedialaw/podcast1-23-uk-media-law

1.24 PAYMENTS TO WITNESSES, CRIMINALS, REPORTING CRIME, AND 'CHEQUE-BOOK JOURNALISM'

There is a secondary media law prohibition on making payments to or offering payments to witnesses in criminal proceedings once they are active under the 1981 Contempt of Court Act and until they are over. This applies to print/online journalists as well as broadcasters. There is a public interest exemption where the proceedings are not yet active, but are likely and foreseeable and if arrangements are entered into, there must be no conditions on the outcome of the trial and the witnesses must be informed that if they are cited to give evidence, the fact of the payment will be disclosed to the prosecution and defence. The PCC has condemned approaching witnesses with offers of payment while they are giving evidence and indeed such conduct could be construed as a possible contempt of court.

> See PCC rulings:
> PCC investigation, *Full House Magazine* (Report 73, 2008)
> http://www.pcc.org.uk/news/index.html?article=NTExNw
> PCC investigation into *News of the World* (Report 63, 2003)
> http://www.pcc.org.uk/news/index.html?article=MjEwNA

There is an ethical obligation to avoid exploiting, glorifying or glamorizing crime in general, and payments to criminals, their family, friends and colleagues can only be entered into if there are good reasons to support the public interest. The PCC has indicated quite strongly that they would not recognize public interest in making entertainment about crime narratives, the kiss-and-tell dimension of romance or sex associated with the narrative or 'irrelevant gossip, which intrudes on the privacy of others'. The same rules apply to broadcasters subject to Ofcom and BBC regulation. For example, sections 3.1 and 3.2 of the Ofcom Code stipulate: 'Material likely to encourage or incite the commission of crime or to lead to disorder must not be included in television or radio services. […] Descriptions or demonstrations of criminal techniques which contain essential details which could enable the commission of crime must not be broadcast unless editorially justified.' There has to be a likelihood of encouragement or incitement, and filming of a criminal activity is not in itself a breach of the rule. The Ofcom ban on paying criminals and their relatives and friends to take part in programmes about their crimes is underpinned by its recognition of the legal constraints imposed on convicted criminals under the Proceeds of Crime Act 2002, to prevent criminals from benefiting from their crimes. However, Ofcom recognizes that the rule should not prevent reformed criminals developing a new career in the media as a process of rehabilitation. Furthermore, payments are acceptable if they amount to 'legitimate expenses reasonably incurred in the production or pre-production of a programme or part of programme; for example, travel and subsistence'.

The PCC has adjudicated against a newspaper that published an article about a mother who justified her behaviour after she was convicted of having unlawful sex with her teenage son. But the PCC rejected a complaint about a payment to a petty criminal who described the presence of the Lord Chief Justice conducting research into community service.

The BBC has a very detailed framework of guidelines that their employees are obliged to comply with in 'reporting crime and anti-social behaviour'. Anybody as a BBC employee, freelance or independent producer must read and understand the 'mandatory referral' requirements for working in this area: http://www.bbc.co.uk/editorialguidelines/page/guidelines-crime-mandatory-referrals. In addition to the sirens recognized by the PCC and Ofcom, you should be aware of additional problem issues that include: witnessing serious criminal activity as a reporter; interviewing criminal fugitives; entering UK or foreign prisons without the permission of the authorities; interviewing or permitting the live broadcast of prisoners; naming or identifying convicted paedophiles/sex offenders when the information has not been released by the police; granting anonymity to law-breakers; hiring convicted criminals; hiring undercover operatives; recording the unlawful harming of animals; suspicions of online grooming of children; identifying anyone aged 17 and under accused in the courts of a criminal offence; investigating crime or anti-social behaviour; using covert surveillance/recording techniques; and/or confronting 'terrorists, serious criminal or extremist or violent political groups'. The BBC sets out a policy position in relation to reporting crime with a commitment to 'giving audiences the facts in their context' and that their reporting 'must not add to people's fear of becoming victims of crime if statistics suggest it is very unlikely'. In short the BBC appears to expect its journalists not to exploit the narrative of real crime cases in order to make entertainment by giving people nightmares and more particularly 'seek to balance the public interest in reporting crime with respect for the privacy and dignity of victims and their families'.

See PCC rulings:
Moffat MP v *Chat* magazine (Report 73, 2006)
http://www.pcc.org.uk/news/index.html?article=MzkzNw
Thames Valley Probation Area v *Mail on Sunday* (Report 74, 2007)
http://www.pcc.org.uk/news/index.html?article=NDIyOA
Ms Christine Wishart v *Take a Break* (Report 79, 2009)
http://www.pcc.org.uk/news/index.html?article=NTczMA
McInnes v *Daily Record* (Report 62, 2003)
http://www.pcc.org.uk/news/index.html?article=MjEwMA
Ofcom Broadcasting Code section 3 Crime guidance
http://stakeholders.ofcom.org.uk/binaries/broadcast/guidance/831193/section3.pdf
BBC Editorial Guidelines. Section 8: Reporting Crime and Anti-Social Behaviour
http://www.bbc.co.uk/editorialguidelines/page/guidance-crime-full

---

★ A downloadable sound file on this section dealing with the issue of cheque-book journalism and sensationalizing crime narratives.
1.24 podcast downloadable https://soundcloud.com/comparativemedialaw/podcast1-24-uk-media-law

1.25 ETHICAL OBLIGATIONS IN RELATION TO KIDNAPPING AND HOSTAGE-TAKING NEWS STORIES

Section 3.6 of the Ofcom Code states that broadcasters 'must use their best endeavours so as not to broadcast material that could endanger lives or prejudice the success of attempts to deal with a hijack or kidnapping'. Although the PCC Code does not address this issue, it has been a long-standing tradition and ethic since 1975 that media organizations cooperate with police enquiries into kidnappings where they observe a news blackout in return for briefings on the development of the investigation and media access to people if and when the victims have been released into safety. This degree of cooperation is encouraged by the UK Society of Editors and ACPO, the Association of Chief Police Officers. The Ofcom Code is designed to ensure that there is no live coverage of events that could assist hostage-takers to frustrate rescue attempts. One really cannot think of any journalist who would rather their competitive ambition clumsily risk the life and safety of a kidnapping or hostage victim. However, state authorities and media need to be cautious about the circumstances of agreed news blackouts. The arrangement relating to Prince Harry's deployment on active military service to Afghanistan in 2008 became controversial. The BBC has a detailed section on 'Hijacking, Kidnapping, Hostage Taking and Sieges' in its Editorial Guidelines. Of particular importance is the prohibition on interviewing perpetrators live on air, or broadcasting any video and/or audio provided by a perpetrator live on air. The transmission of any recordings made by perpetrators requires referral to a senior editorial figure or commissioning editor in the case of independents. The BBC also has a policy of using a delay device when taking live feeds from 'sensitive stories, for example a school siege or plane hijack'. BBC employees must check their obligations for mandatory referrals to senior editorial figures, commissioning editors and Director of Editorial Policy in relation to issues of 'War, Terror and Emergencies': http://www.bbc.co.uk/editorialguidelines/page/guidelines-war-mandatory-referrals.

BBC Editorial Guidelines: 'Hijacking, Kidnapping, Hostage Taking and Sieges'
http://www.bbc.co.uk/editorialguidelines/page/guidelines-war-practices-hijacking/
The News Manual. Prince Harry in Afghanistan
http://www.thenewsmanual.net/Resources/whats_new_in_news01.htm

☆ A downloadable sound file on this section concerning the ethics of reporting sieges and hostage-taking.
1.25 podcast downloadable https://soundcloud.com/comparativemedialaw/podcast1-25-uk-media-law

1.26 UPDATES AND STOP PRESS

British media law changes, sometimes week by week. This book's companion website gives you a direct link to updates, developments and information you need to know that has emerged after the book's print publication.

http://www.ma-radio.gold.ac.uk/medialawpocketbook/contemptupdates

Other laws concerning anonymity, privacy and secret hearings (excluding media and public) are dealt with in later chapters. Differences and issues relating specifically to Scotland and Northern Ireland are dealt with in Chapter 8.

Key general links
Glossary of legal terms in United Kingdom
http://www.judiciary.gov.uk/glossary
BBC College of Journalism guidance on Contempt and Reporting Restrictions
http://www.bbc.co.uk/academy/collegeofjournalism/law/contempt/contempt-and-reporting-restrictions

Key general links *continued*
Ofcom Broadcasting Code February 2011
http://stakeholders.ofcom.org.uk/binaries/broadcast/831190/
broadcastingcode2011.pdf
BBC Editorial Guidelines
http://www.bbc.co.uk/editorialguidelines/
BBC College of Journalism online guidance on editorial standards
http://www.bbc.co.uk/academy/collegeofjournalism/standards
UK Press Complaints Commission
http://www.pcc.org.uk/

BBC Trust Complaints, appeals and other findings: all complaints to the BBC are first dealt with by the BBC Complaints Unit which publishes a very brief monthly summary at: http://www.bbc.co.uk/complaints/reports/

Editorial Standards Committee run by the BBC Trust hears appeals about BBC management's decisions on editorial complaints about editorial content in actual BBC programmes or online content:

http://www.bbc.co.uk/bbctrust/our_work/complaints_and_appeals/
esc.html
The Trust also adjudicates on complaints about other issues:
http://www.bbc.co.uk/bbctrust/our_work/complaints_and_appeals/
UK Society of Editors downloads of guides and resources for
journalists and broadcasters:
http://www.societyofeditors.co.uk/page-view.
php?pagename=Reportsandguides
The Report of the Leveson Inquiry into the Culture, Practice and Ethics
of the Press
http://www.levesoninquiry.org.uk/about/the-report/

✱ A downloadable sound file on this section concerning updates to the law of media contempt and reporting crime.
1.26 Podcast downloadable https://soundcloud.com/comparativemedialaw/podcast1-26-uk-media-law

2

GUIDE TO COURT REPORTING
– KEY FACTS AND CHECKLIST

Key rules and professional standards when court reporting in 16 bullet points:

- Attribution, facts not comment, avoid adjectives and adverbs unless attributed and obtain full contacts – first and last names, age, living, address, telephone, mobile and email
- Respectfully dressed and respectfully behaved
- Information preparation, check your technology and reconnaissance
- Availability of agreed prosecution opening, skeleton arguments, CPS-media protocol, reporting from crime locations, reconstructions and court visits to the scenes of crime
- Reporting restrictions – children, sex offence complainants, vulnerable witnesses, reporting postponement orders etc: always check
- Names of protagonists, their titles and proper terminology – background briefing on legal system and how it works

- Understanding the trial/case structure and narrative
- Ban on cameras on precincts, permission only to use sound recording, caution over tweeting – allowed but can be banned, keep two notes going
- Accuracy paramount, keep to vocabulary used in court, establish intro and angle and avoid over-complicating the plot
- Fairness paramount in every report – always include something on each side, no opinions or comment, only assert facts not in dispute, attribute everything else
- Never live broadcast/report without preparing script and notes and working off these
- No reporting of anything in the absence of the jury
- Interviews with judges, counsel, jurors not allowed – witnesses, police officers and instructing solicitors/crown prosecutors possible – usually outside the court
- Extreme caution over interviews with anonymous witnesses subject to reporting restrictions
- Press conferences where people are interviewed collectively (even impromptu on the pavement outside the court building) and all media have access carry qualified privilege for libel subject to explanation or contradiction – single one-to-one interviews do not
- Keep your notes, files and papers

★ A downloadable sound file of bullet point professional tips and rules for court reporting.
2.0 podcast downloadable https://soundcloud.com/comparativemedialaw/chapter2bulletpooints-uk-media

A short video-cast explaining key UK media law points on court reporting
2. video-cast http://youtu.be/RV1VL2jOt1c

2.1   ATTRIBUTION, FACTS NOT COMMENT ETC

Your mind needs to concentrate on the basics of journalism: who, what, why, where, when and how. Always attribute; facts not comments from you as the reporter; park your politics and personal prejudices at home; fairness and accuracy are your priority; proper spellings; first and last names of participants in your story, the proper pronunciation of their names; their age (date of birth means you can calibrate their age in later reports); what they do for a living; where they live – including specific house/flat number; work and out-of-work contact numbers – landlines and mobile; email addresses.

☆   A downloadable sound file on this section emphasizing attribution and avoiding comment.
2.1 Podcast downloadable https://soundcloud.com/comparativemedialaw/podcast2-1-uk-media-law

2.2   RESPECTFULLY DRESSED AND RESPECTFULLY BEHAVED

Respectfully dressed and respectfully behaved. Court hearings involve protagonists who are under great stress; crimes involve traumatic and catastrophic events that are intensely emotional; legal hearings have rituals that are similar to religious services. There is also a dreadful social and unjustifiable prejudice against journalists whipped up by politicians and scriptwriters, which means you will be judged and watched much more harshly than other people in the process.

☆   A downloadable sound file stressing the need for respectful presentation and behaviour.
2.2 Podcast downloadable https://soundcloud.com/comparativemedialaw/podcast2-2-uk-media-law

2.3 INFORMATION PREPARATION: CHECK YOUR TECHNOLOGY AND RECONNAISSANCE

Prepare your technology and resources of information. Have you a cuttings file from agencies and previous publications informing you of the context and the nature of the hearing? Have you made contact with the court to confirm timing, location, access etc? Better still, have you done a reconnaissance, particularly if you have multi-media requirements? What are the protocols on where you can take pictures and film people entering and leaving in terms of court precincts? Have you established the nature of media facilities, is there a media room, is there a liaison agency journalist who can assist you who is a freelance for your media organization? Have you the basic details of the court parties, number of courtroom, name of judge/justices, sheriff, contacts for the prosecution (police or HM Revenue & Customs), defence solicitors? If you have electronic media equipment, where can you store it while the hearing is in process? If necessary investigate whether you can make an arrangement with a local business in return for a modest/nominal fee. Make sure your mobile/BlackBerry, palm-top and laptop computers are charged up and operational and investigate Wi-Fi and mains connections and access. If you need to have professional-quality sound recordings, consider using a unidirectional 'gun-microphone' that can pick up a bright clear voice signal from a distance of 15 to 20 feet. This is useful if in a high-profile case somebody making a statement is kept distant from a media cordon with the journalists 'marshalled' behind a barrier.

✶ A downloadable sound file on how to get ready for your visit to court.
2.3 Podcast downloadable https://soundcloud.com/comparativemedialaw/podcast2-3-uk-media-law

2.4 AVAILABILITY OF AGREED PROSECUTION OPENING, SKELETON ARGUMENTS ETC

In high-profile cases where the prosecution opening script had been agreed and approved with the defence (in the sense that the defence were assured that the prosecution would not be making any allegations not supported by evidence) photocopies would occasionally be made available to reporters to support accuracy and on the condition that nothing would be reported until it had been spoken in open court and any variations in the live proceedings formed the record and would need to be taken down. Unfortunately a practice developed where many court cases would require paper skeleton arguments from lawyers in order to save time, these would be referred to by way of discussion and argument but not made available to the media reporting the case. In a significant ruling against the concealment from the media of such material at an extradition hearing, the English Court of Appeal in 2012 made it clear that the courts should assist rather than impede access to documents read as evidence. Lord Justice Toulson said:

> The courts have recognized that the practice of receiving evidence without it being read in open court potentially has the side effect of making the proceedings less intelligible to the press and the public. This calls for counter measures. [...] In a case where documents have been placed before a judge and referred to in the course of proceedings, in my judgment the default position should be that access should be permitted on the open justice principle; and where access is sought for a proper journalistic purpose, the case for allowing it will be particularly strong.

> *Guardian News and Media Ltd, R (on the application of) v City of Westminster Magistrates' Court* [2012] EWCA Civ 420 (3 April 2012)
> http://www.bailii.org/ew/cases/EWCA/Civ/2012/420.html

It is also useful to be aware that Rule 5.8 of the Criminal Procedure Rules 2011 provides a procedure for people connected with and interested in court cases, including reporters who want to inspect or copy a document.

Before and during a criminal case a special agreement and arrangement between the CPS and media enables the release of multi-media exhibits in the form of stills, CCTV, video and sound etc where there is no dispute about it being adduced as evidence.

Publicity and the Criminal Justice System: Protocol for working together: Chief Police Officers, Chief Crown Prosecutors and the Media
http://www.cps.gov.uk/publications/agencies/mediaprotocol.html

---

The clichéd style of having a reporter standing outside court on television speaking to the camera can be broken up by finding more interesting locations and angles to the court building from higher buildings nearby. It might also be possible to do some of the pieces from the location of the crime set out in the narrative, though caution and legal advice should be sought, particularly if the court believes the jury's understanding of locations should only be derived from photographs and images presented in court. No attempt, under any circumstances, should be made to simulate or dramatize allegations and evidence while a trial is in progress. Other more imaginative and modern methods of reporting of court cases engage artistic sketching, and computer-generated imagery (CGI) – a process that Sky News and ITV news have certainly pioneered and developed in recent years.

One vital rule in relation to the use of images is that they should not form part of any reporting if they prejudice eyewitness identification in the trial and the risk of this happening needs to be clarified soon after arrest, charge and first court appearances. In Scotland, ordinarily any image representation of the accused is likely to be considered contempt because of the tradition of evidential dock identification in the Scottish legal system.

★   A downloadable sound file on media access to court documents and media release of exhibits for publication. 2.4 Podcast downloadable https://soundcloud.com/comparativemedialaw/podcast2-4-uk-media-law

2.5 REPORTING RESTRICTIONS – CHILDREN, SEX OFFENCE COMPLAINANTS

Establish the nature of any reporting restrictions: young people aged 17 and under (section 39 orders under Children and Young Persons' Act 1933) (16 and under in Scotland); complainants of sexual offences (statutory anonymity); vulnerable witnesses or undercover state investigators; postponement of reporting restrictions because of later trials/cases (section 4(2) orders Contempt of Court Act (CCA) 1981); blackmail complainants where the menaces are embarrassing (common law right); specific orders on identities withheld from the public before the court (section 11 orders CCA 1981). Remember that when you are at the hearing you often hear the names and identifying characteristics of people who have to be legally anonymous in your reports – such as sexual offence complainants and children. It is a paradox of 'open justice' that the public attending the hearing will know that which you as the media are prevented from disseminating. There may be very exceptional situations where witnesses and defendants have pseudonyms – usually in trials connected with gang culture or organized crime, or the secret services. It will be a very serious criminal offence if you publicly report the measures that have been taken to protect the witnesses and risk of prejudice and security in these circumstances.

✳   A downloadable sound file summarizing your need to check reporting restrictions.
2.5 Podcast downloadable https://soundcloud.com/comparativemedialaw/podcast2-5-uk-media-law

2.6 NAMES OF PROTAGONISTS, THEIR TITLES AND PROPER TERMINOLOGY ETC

Identify the names of the prosecuting counsel/advocates (first and second names) and their status – are they QCs or not? The same in relation to defence counsel/advocates. What is the proper title of the judge and any variants, first and second name? District Judge, Judge, Mr or Mrs Justice, Lord Justice (usually male or female), Lord or Supreme Court Justice etc? What is the name of the court? Is it a magistrates' court, sheriff court, Crown Court, High Court, Appeal Court, Employment Tribunal or Supreme Court? Try to ensure that you understand and use the terminology correctly. In criminal trials sitting with juries, it is the juries who decide the facts in issue and return a verdict, not the judge, who only does the sentencing. In England the lawyers doing the pleading and advocacy are usually barristers or the more senior ones will have been appointed Queen's Counsel (QCs). They will be known as King's Counsel if the reigning monarch is male. In some courts the case may be presented by a solicitor-advocate. Usually solicitors are the instructing lawyers who have prepared the case. In Scotland the criminal cases are prepared and presented by the Procurator Fiscal. In England and Wales this is done by the CPS who prosecute the case on behalf of the police. Jurors are 'sworn in' when criminal defendants plead not guilty. There are 12 in England and Wales and 15 in Scotland. In England and Wales the verdicts are either guilty or not guilty, but in Scotland there is a third verdict 'not proven'. Majorities, on the direction of the judge, are permitted in England on the basis of 10–2, 11–1 or, if jurors are discharged through illness or other reasons, 10–1. In Scotland majority verdicts are more flexible and can be 8–7. You also need to appreciate that the prosecution's opening speech, usually the most common and popularly reported sequence of any criminal trial, is only a series of allegations (which has to be supported by the evidence the prosecution intend to call) and in attribution your use of the verb 'allege' would be sensible.

★   A downloadable sound file on reporting names and titles when covering criminal trials.
      2.6 Podcast downloadable https://soundcloud.com/comparativemedialaw/podcast2-6-uk-media-law

2.7   UNDERSTANDING THE TRIAL/CASE STRUCTURE AND NARRATIVE

The sequence of trial process usually works on the basis of indictment/charges laid against the defendant, pleas taken, jury selected and sworn in, prosecution opening speech, witness called to give evidence, 'opened' by the prosecution (leading questions not usually permitted) cross-examination by the defence, and re-examination if new issues are raised by defence cross-examination. The defence case rarely begins with an opening speech. It tends to start by calling witnesses and usually the defendant is the first witness to be called if he/she intends to give evidence. The testimony is 'opened' by the defence counsel, and cross-examined by the prosecution and/or co-defendants. Re-examination follows if new issues are raised by cross-examination, followed by the prosecution final speech, defence final speech, summing up by the judge, jury deliberation and verdicts. The prosecution will 'open' the facts on any matter to which the defendant previously pleaded guilty, take evidence about 'antecedents' or previous convictions of the defendant usually by evidence from the senior investigating police officer. The court can also receive a witness or victim impact statement which is a summary of the effects of the crime on the victim and/or family, a 'pre-sentence' report from the probation service if the court is considering non-custodial sentencing and/or the judge wants information about the social circumstances of the defendant, and a 'medical report' from a forensic psychiatrist or psychiatrists about the defendant's mental health. Finally, the court would hear a plea of mitigation by the defence lawyer before sentencing by the judge. There are exceptions and variations to this structure. If a defendant(s) pleads guilty and this is accepted by the prosecution, the structure will proceed directly to the stage at which the prosecution 'opens' the case with an agreed narrative of the facts that are not in dispute. Trial structure and ritual in Scotland have some notable differences because it is a different legal jurisdiction. For example, there is no opening speech by the prosecution.

★ A downloadable sound file on understanding how a criminal trial proceeds.
2.7 Podcast downloadable https://soundcloud.com/comparativemedialaw/podcast2-7-uk-media-law

2.8 CAMERAS, RECORDING AND TWEETING

Do not use a camera on the precincts or inside the courtrooms, do not make sketches, do not make sound recordings (you might be given permission for sound recording for note-taking purposes). The situation may change when television cameras are allowed in as a matter of practice. For example, trial judges may well permit multi-media reporters and photographers the opportunity of taking stills inside the courtroom of the judge and lawyers who will be 'viewable'. If these photo-calls are not allowed, arrangements may well be possible for screen grabs from the television coverage. Having good and practised shorthand at 100 words per minute minimum will be most useful – perhaps it is an old skill not supported and appreciated enough in contemporary journalism. Keep a note going of what is happening while it is happening and run a separate note constructing your copy while you are in the courtroom. This is very useful if you have to file regular reports. Have an arrangement with another journalist you can trust who will cover for you while you have to leave the courtroom for bathroom or filing purposes. Tweet with extreme caution. Only transmit what you would normally file, though some experienced court reporters are getting many followers by including colour and information that is of interest to people involved in the legal system as much as the public outside.

> At the time of writing see Jason Evans:
> http://twitter.com/evansthecrime
> Rob Middleton:
> http://twitter.com/robmiddleton23
> You can see how the *Guardian* reporter Steven Morris tweeted from the Vincent Tabak trial for the murder of Joanna Yeates:
> http://www.guardian.co.uk/twitter/list/JoYeatesTrial
> He also wrote an interesting feature article on the experience:
> http://www.guardian.co.uk/uk/2011/nov/02/vincent-tabak-trial-tweeted

Remember: even deleted tweets are still in the public domain – for example they cannot be deleted from Facebook feeds. Errors in immediate tweeting in a process of 'live' court reporting place you and your publisher at risk of committing serious criminal offences. However, tweeting is becoming a new phenomenon in the open justice process whereby concise and abbreviated tweetscourtspeak is becoming an effective way of reporting cases at all levels.

> At the time of writing a news agency covering London's Central Criminal Court and other court buildings offered a regular feed of tweets from newsworthy cases
> http://twitter.com/CourtNewsUK
> 'News reports from the Old Bailey, London's Crown Courts and UK disciplinary hearings'
> http://www.courtnewsuk.co.uk

✻   A downloadable sound file on the use of cameras, sound recorders, mini-computer and social media transmission devices in the courtroom.
2.8 Podcast downloadable https://soundcloud.com/comparativemedialaw/podcast2-8-uk-media-law

2.9 ACCURACY PARAMOUNT

In the writing of your report(s) establish the intro first based on the best possible news angle and then within the frame of that report write a narrative consistently focusing on that angle or plot. Court reporting is a balance between clarifying and explaining a complicated legal process and an accurate and fair representation of it. The storytelling needs to be interesting and to some extent might even be 'entertaining' in order to maintain the attention of your audience. In law the construction of the story always has to remain accurate and 'fair'. To achieve a high index of accuracy, it is best to concentrate solely on facts that are not in dispute in the adversarial proceedings, and then always to attribute assertions and submissions. Only report what is being stated within the court proceedings and use neutral language in attribution. 'Claimed' suggests something is being asserted with doubt attached to it, whereas 'said' and 'submitted' does not carry any charged meaning. Avoid adjectives and adverbs unless they are used by the witnesses and protagonists you are quoting.

* A downloadable sound file on how to maintain accuracy when reporting court cases.
  2.9 Podcast downloadable https://soundcloud.com/comparativemedialaw/podcast2-9-uk-media-law

2.10 FAIRNESS PARAMOUNT

Full fairness cannot be guaranteed in every report; particularly where the focus may be on the prosecution or the defence, but in every report you must state the position of the other side; for example that they are pleading not guilty to the specific charges and that the trial is continuing. Fairness needs to be fulfilled for the entire reporting of a case by ensuring that your publisher covers the result. It does not mean that you have to have a proportionate amount of time and space devoted to the reporting of prosecution/defence and claimant/defendant, but obviously you will expose yourself to the criticism that your reporting is 'unfair' if nothing or significantly very little of either side is included. Serious problems could arise if you report a powerful allegation being made and then omit the rebuttal or reply in court, particularly if made during the same day's proceedings. Be cautious about paraphrasing the narrative of a court case. It is advisable to use only the words used in court or vocabulary very close in meaning to the words used. You should never, under any circumstances, comment on or express opinions about the evidence or performance of the protagonists or make predictions on the relative merits of the parties. Court reporting is not sports reporting, nor a review of a Hollywood film or play in the West End.

* A downloadable sound recording on how to maintain fairness when court reporting.
  2.10 Podcast downloadable https://soundcloud.com/comparativemedialaw/podcast2-10-uk-media-law

2.11 USE NOTES/SCRIPTS FOR LIVE BROADCASTS

If you are live broadcasting, it is highly advisable that you script your material beforehand and only agree to 'ad libbing' or reporting extempore when you are very experienced or at least when a case is completed. The risk of doing so during the trial is that you could mistakenly commit a contempt of court that leads to a case being halted, and the risk of doing so post-trial is that you could inadvertently libel somebody because a combination of inaccuracy and unfairness vitiates your absolute and qualified privilege for libel.

★   A downloadable sound file on best practice when 'live reporting' from court cases.
2.11 Podcast downloadable https://soundcloud.com/comparativemedialaw/podcast2-11-uk-media-law

2.12 IN THE ABSENCE OF THE JURY USUALLY REPORT NOTHING

There is a golden rule that nothing should be reported that is in the absence of a jury. If the jury are sent out of the courtroom it is normally because the trial judge will be discussing a matter that is or could be prejudicial and it is something that the jury should not know. Usually courts make almost default postponing orders on publication for mid-trial proceedings with the jury absent, but even if they do not, it is wholly advisable not to immediately report what has happened before obtaining legal advice.

★   A downloadable sound file on the need to avoid contemporaneous reporting of absence of the jury hearings.
2.12 Podcast downloadable https://soundcloud.com/comparativemedialaw/podcast2-12-uk-media-law

2.13   INTERVIEWS – JUDGES AND JURORS NO, OTHERS BE CAREFUL WHERE AND HOW

Do not attempt to interview the judges or jurors – interviewing the latter is likely to be a contempt of court and would probably lead to immediate arrest. Professional rules mean that representing counsel – barristers, QCs and advocates – cannot do on-the-record interviews. Police officers, instructing solicitors, witnesses, defendants whether acquitted or convicted (when receiving non-custodial sentences) and relatives of people involved may be interviewed, usually off the premises of the court, though print/online reporters can often carry out interviews inside the public areas of the court building. Remember that if you interview victims/witnesses, reporting restrictions/anonymity provisions could apply. Where the anonymity is statutory and written consent to identification is not given, avoid any identifying details (remember the information could be something that somebody they know well could link to them). In electronic media only use actors or other reporters to voice up the script – concealing voice distortion software does not work and conversion programmes are easily available online. Remember despite visual concealment, interviewees can still be identified by silhouette, hairstyle, and unique physical movements etc.

★   A downloadable sound file on reasons to be careful when approaching and interviewing people involved in criminal trials.
2.13 Podcast downloadable https://soundcloud.com/comparativemedialaw/podcast2-13-uk-media-law

2.14   QUALIFIED PRIVILEGE AT PRESS CONFERENCES – USEFUL

In post-trial interviews remember that you will be able to rely on qualified privilege against libel, subject to explanation or contradiction, if they are conducted in the context of a press conference to which any media have access and this can happen on the street/pavement outside the court building. This means that the statement made and questions asked are collective by way of a public meeting. One-to-one interviews are unlikely to be privileged.

✱ A downloadable sound file explaining how post-trial press conferences, like public meetings, have qualified privilege for libel.
2.14 Podcast downloadable https://soundcloud.com/comparativemedialaw/podcast2-14-uk-media-law

2.15 KEEP YOUR NOTES AND CASE PAPERS

Always keep your notes and background papers on any cases you report for up to six years after the event. There is a case for keeping them until you retire. This is because libel hearings can be brought within one year of publication (three years in Scotland) and the information may be of use in future reporting. There may be circumstances when future reporters for your publication need to consult you about the case. The defendant or parties to the case may be involved in future cases or news events, or be at the centre of a miscarriage of justice campaign and appealing against the conviction and sentence.

Systematic and extensive filing of information about living people in the form of a near library and/or electronic databases from your reporting may require notification to the Information Commissioner under the 1998 Data Protection Act. The IO states categorically that if you are doing so for the purposes of journalism and media 'You are required to notify unless you are a not-for-profit organisation.'

Notifications Exemptions: A Self-Assessment Guide from the Information Officer's Office
http://www.ico.gov.uk/~/media/documents/library/Data_Protection/Forms/notification_exemptions_-_self-assessment_guide.ashx

---

It would seem journalists are not exempt from registering with the IO, but they do enjoy an exemption from any demand to see the information they are holding if the data is held and processed 'only for journalistic, literary or artistic purposes' or 'only for research, statistical or historical purposes'. Fears have been expressed that proposals in the Leveson Inquiry Report of 2012 would weaken the protection to journalists currently afforded by section 32 of the Act.

Section 32 Data Protection Act 1998 Journalism, literature and art.
http://www.legislation.gov.uk/ukpga/1998/29/section/32
Leveson and data protection – a hidden threat
http://www.holdthefrontpage.co.uk/2012/news/
leveson-and-data-protection-%E2%80%93-a-hidden-threat/

In 2008 a freelance photographer was prosecuted and fined nearly £1,000 for failing to register.

'Data Protection Requires' NUJ London Freelance Branch Newsletter
September 2008
http://www.londonfreelance.org/fl/0809dpa.html

The cost of annual registration is at the time of writing £35 for individual journalists and/or organizations with a turnover of less than £25.9 million and 250 or more members of staff.

Information Commissioner's Office FAQs on the need to register
(notify) under Data Protection Act
http://www.ico.gov.uk/for_organisations/data_protection/notification.
aspx

☆   A downloadable sound file advising on the keeping of notes and records.
2.15 Podcast downloadable https://soundcloud.com/comparativemedialaw/podcast2-15-uk-media-law

2.16 MORE INFORMATION AND BACKGROUND, STOP PRESS AND UPDATES

For a more comprehensive guide to court reporting consult the chapter 'Court Reporting: Courts, Inquests, Tribunals, Inquiries' in *Essential Reporting: The NCTJ Guide for Trainee Journalists* by Jon Smith, 2011, published by Sage, pages 173–92. For more comprehensive and detailed information on reporting the Scottish legal system consult *Scots Law for Journalists* edited by Rosalind McInnes, 8th edition 2010, published by W. Green. For a guide on the Scottish legal system see *Scottish Legal System Essentials* by Bryan Clark, 2nd edition 2009, published by Dundee University Press.

'English Legal System Overview' – sample chapter from *English Legal System Directions* by Steve Wilson, Rebecca Mitchell, Tony Storey, and Natalie Wortley, 2nd edition 2011, Oxford University Press
http://www.oup.com/uk/orc/bin/9780199592241/wilson2e_ch01.pdf
UK Ministry of Justice online guide to legal system in England and Wales
http://open.justice.gov.uk/courts/
'About the Scottish Courts' from the Scottish Courts website maintained by the Scottish Government.
http://www.scotcourts.gov.uk/about.asp

★ A downloadable sound file on this section pointing to useful books and sources and summarizing updates on the practice of court reporting.
2.16 Podcast downloadable https://soundcloud.com/comparativemedialaw/podcast2-16-uk-media-law

3

LIBEL, PRIVACY, ACCURACY AND BALANCE

Key bullet points setting out legal duties in relation to libel, privacy, accuracy and balance:

- Libel is inaccurate publication that does serious harm to reputation and can attract civil litigation with huge costs and economic damage to the publisher. The burden of proof is not on the claimant but on the defendant publisher. Defences include 'responsible journalism' in the public interest, absolute and qualified privilege in fair and accurate reports of court proceedings, public meetings, press conferences, parliamentary and local government proceedings, and the publications of government bodies; innocent dissemination; justification also known as 'truth', and honest comment
- Breach of privacy is a civil wrong, a failure to respect the right to privacy of an individual (as defined by Article 8 of the 1998 Human Rights Act (HRA) and European Convention on Human Rights (ECHR)), and is usually

a truthful publication, though can also be untruthful, and can include conduct that is intrusive and does not lead to any publication. The victim must have a 'reasonable expectation of privacy' and media breaches of that privacy must be 'in the public interest'. Most legal actions involve interim prior restraint injunctions, though the few that have gone to full trial involve the award of damages (highest at the time of writing is £60,000) and legal costs, which are much more substantial

- Privacy as a concept is also recognized in secondary media law and it can be argued that the case histories of the Press Complaints Commission and future independent regulation of the press industry give a much more practical guide to the ethics of professional boundaries than legal precedent. Privacy is also defined and applied in the Ofcom Broadcasting Code and BBC Editorial Guidelines

- Inaccurate speech that neither harms reputation nor breaches privacy can be a breach of secondary media law in terms of the Ofcom Code, BBC Editorial Guidelines and independent press regulation (previously PCC Code of Practice). The regulatory remedy for inaccuracy can include published correction, apology, provision of right to reply, critical adjudication and fines. Ofcom has additional power to suspend and delete the licences of broadcasters

- Publications deemed to be 'unfair' and/or causing 'harm and offence' are recognized in broadcasting as a breach of regulation. Such publications do not usually breach primary media law

- In broadcasting, publications deemed to be impartial and giving undue prominence of views and opinions are also constructed as breaches of regulation. Biased and partial publications in print and online are not breaches of any primary or secondary media law, though the

Code of Practice did require the press to 'distinguish clearly between comment, conjecture and fact' and this ethical aspiration is expected to be followed by its successor regulator

★ A downloadable sound file voicing bullet points that summarize libel, privacy and the regulation of accuracy and balance.
3.0 Podcast downloadable https://soundcloud.com/comparativemedialaw/chapter-3-bullet-points-libel

A short video-cast explaining key UK media law points on libel, privacy, accuracy and balance.
3. video-cast http://youtu.be/oBq6CXeLHOc

3.1 LIBEL AND PRIVACY – THE CHILLING EFFECT

Defamation, generally known and defined in journalism law as 'libel', carries civil law sanctions such as being sued for high damages and having to pay lawyers huge amounts in fees. A research study in 2008 demonstrated that lawyers in England charge 140 times more than in other European countries. There was political consensus in 2011 that the success fee uplifts of up to 100% for the lawyers representing successful media libel and privacy litigants should be substantially cut back, including the recommendation of a report drawn up by an Appeal Court judge. These reforms will come into force in April 2013 and restrict success fees to a maximum proportion of 25% of damages. The UK government would not settle a successful action brought by Mirror Group Newspapers at the European Court of Human Rights (ECtHR) in 2011 that ruled the near one million pounds in legal fees for losing the privacy action against model Naomi Campbell amounted to a breach of Article 10 freedom of expression. In 2012 the Strasbourg Court ordered the government to pay more than £200,000 in damages to MGN. The 2012 Leveson Inquiry Report recommended that exemplary damages (punitive and deterrent) should be extended from libel to all civil wrongs in journalism conduct and publication including privacy, and if implemented this may lead to the inflation of awards.

Libel and privacy are highly complex areas of media law and the summaries in this book can only be regarded as a simple guide. If you receive a legal complaint, it is essential that you take professional and specialist advice. The precedents referred to can only be seen as relating to the specific facts of each case. In English law, lawyers are expert at 'distinguishing' cases so that the law of precedent has a tendency to have a very limited impact. It is also often the case that attempts by Parliament to codify or 'simplify' media law only succeed in becoming substantially complicated by case law.

In practice UK media publishers exercise caution to avoid legal trouble and potential litigants know this. Most cases are settled because the costs of defending them greatly outweigh the risk and benefits of succeeding.

At the time of writing the British newspaper tabloid tradition of 'kiss-and-tell' stories about the private lives of celebrities and politicians has withered and an examination of a successfully defended action such as *Ferdinand v MGN* in 2011 yields a judgment with the word 'redacted' used 20 times. It is likely that the costs of legally defending privacy litigation over a story that is merely entertaining and/or dealing with the moral character of a public figure vastly outweighs the benefits in publication, even when it might be proved to be in the public interest. This climate of self-censorship and caution by media publishers in the face of claimant-friendly media law is known as 'the chilling effect'. The public interest is not determined by journalists or publishers, but by state prosecuting officials, and the judiciary. Juries do not decide the facts in privacy actions and are to be abolished in trials for libel in the 2012 Defamation Bill so it is important to realize that media law in the UK is made and controlled by judiciary, legislature, government, regulatory quango (Ofcom and the BBC Trust), past self-regulation by the PCC and future independent regulation of the press industry in terms of newspapers, magazines, and their associated online sites, and media employers' internal 'readers' editors', ombudspersons and codes of ethics. Cases where media defendants are successful are the exception rather than the rule and in fact the most heroic defence of a libel action in modern times was by two environmental campaigners and non-media professionals who resisted a corporate libel action by McDonald's over critical leaflets they distributed outside the fast food giant's restaurant in Holborn, Central London. The ruling in their favour by the ECtHR in Strasbourg presents a David and Goliath story, yet the UK Parliament has not introduced any reforms to reduce the chilling effect of corporate libel actions.

Steel and Morris v The United Kingdom App no. 68416/01 [2005] ECtHR 103 (15 February 2005)
http://www.bailii.org/eu/cases/ECHR/2005/103.html

In December 2011 the ECtHR approved the award of 35,000 euros non-pecuniary damages and over 47,000 euros in costs and expenses to Helen Steel and David Morris.

Steel and Morris v The United Kingdom App no. 68416/01 [2011] ECtHR 2272 (2 December 2011)
http://www.bailii.org/eu/cases/ECHR/2011/2272.html
Links
'A Comparative Study of Costs in Defamation Proceedings Across Europe' by Programme in Comparative Media Law and Policy Centre for Socio-Legal Studies University of Oxford, December 2008
http://pcmlp.socleg.ox.ac.uk/sites/pcmlp.socleg.ox.ac.uk/files/defamationreport.pdf
MGN Ltd v United Kingdom App no. 39401/04 [2011] ECtHR 66 (18 January 2011) on Naomi Campbell winning breach of privacy and MGN challenging legal cost regime
http://www.bailii.org/eu/cases/ECHR/2011/66.html
MGN Ltd v United Kingdom App no. 39401/04 [2012] ECtHR 993 (12 June 2012) on damages
http://www.bailii.org/eu/cases/ECHR/2012/993.html

✳   A downloadable sound file on the chilling effect of libel and privacy laws in UK media.
3.1 Podcast downloadable https://soundcloud.com/comparativemedialaw/podcast-3-1-uk-media-law

3.2 LIBEL – DEFAMATION LAW IN DEFINITION AND EXPLANATION

There have been four basic common law definitions of how to measure whether your expression and communication could be libellous:

a   what you write exposes someone to hatred, ridicule and contempt;
b   what you write lowers the estimation of right-thinking people generally;
c   what you write damages someone in their trade, profession or office;
d   what you write causes people to shun and avoid your subject.

The Defamation Bill in 2012 proposed to introduce a statutory requirement that 'publication must have caused serious harm or be likely to cause serious harm to the reputation of the claimant' (section 1). This appears to put into statute the test of 'seriousness' set out in the case of *Thornton v Telegraph Media Group* [2010] EWHC 1414 (QB) (http://www.bailii.org/ew/cases/EWHC/QB/2010/1414.html) and will probably be measured in a claim about the impact of the libel on audience and circulation. There is another form of defamation in England and Wales called 'slander' but this does not usually relate to professional media communication as it is restricted to gestural defamation (being frog-marched or reputation embarrassed by hand or facial expressions) and everyday speech. Most media publication e.g. speech on radio and television, performance in theatre and film, online text and imagery is defined by statute and case law as libel. Slander also has categories requiring proof of special damage e.g. defaming in relation to work, office or profession.

Identification: even if you do not name someone explicitly, if it is possible to work out who you are talking about you can be sued by them. In England and Wales publication has to be to only one third party; not just to newspaper or magazine readership. This means that sending a postcard to one individual with a defamatory comment about another person is sufficient to attract litigation.

My advice in terms of a useful rule to test whether your copy is potentially libellous is to imagine you are the most sensitive person being criticized and think the very worst interpretation of what could be misunderstood by the language you have used in your copy. Remember that if you are sued it will be the judge who determines the potential meaning, not you, and the claimant's lawyers will argue forcefully for the most exaggerated and extreme pejorative interpretation in terms of meaning.

Another method of testing your copy is to think in terms of bane and antidote. Consider the worst possible 'reading' of your material (known as the bane), make your assessment on one quick and immediate reading (the natural and ordinary meaning expected of your audience), then look for any antidote in terms of putting the other side, indicating that the bane is ridiculous, meaningless satire that nobody would believe, and contextualization, which would ensure that any reasonable reader would not derive any defamatory meaning.

When you are writing or broadcasting try to go out of your way to separate fact from comment. This is because facts have to be proved and if defamatory are the most dangerous parts of your copy. Comment should be opinion, honestly held and based on true facts, or allegations made in legally privileged contexts.

Always avoid alleging and/or imputing defamatory motive. Not even the prosecution has to prove motive in a criminal trial. It is almost impossible to prove unless admitted. There is a famous legal quotation about how it is as impossible to guess the state of a man's mind as it would be to guess the state of his digestion. In the current age of new social media and online publication it is important to beware of the risks of innuendo, reasonable inference and jigsaw identification. In 2012 a BBC *Newsnight* programme included untrue allegations about a retired politician without naming him, but his identification on Twitter and online established the connection. The BBC apologized, settled and paid substantial damages. ITV had to apologize and pay damages to the same claimant when a presenter downloaded his name from Internet rumours and this could be seen on a piece of paper handed to the Prime Minister during a live interview. In 2006 the *News of the World* was successfully sued by the soccer player Ashley Cole whose lawyers argued that a libellous article not naming him still led to his identification when read in conjunction with the material naming him on the Internet.

In England and Wales claimants should issue their writs within a year of publication. However, libel law left a continuing jeopardy where a new publication would trigger another year's opportunity for taking action and the courts ruled that online libel would be a new publication whenever it was viewed by anyone. To ensure there is a time limit that can be properly anticipated and applied by media publishers, Parliament has introduced in section 8 of the 2012 Defamation Bill 'the single publication rule'. This will mean that where somebody 'publishes a statement to the public ("the first publication"), and subsequently publishes (whether or not to the public) that statement or a statement which is substantially the same, any cause of action against the person for defamation in respect of the subsequent publication is to be treated as having accrued on the date of the first publication'. Under section 4A of the Limitation Act 1980 the time limit for actions for defamation is one year from the date of first publication. The new legislation states that the first publication rule will not apply if the subsequent 'republication' is 'materially different from the manner of the first publication' and this will be decided on the basis of the 'level of prominence that a statement is given and the extent of the subsequent publication'. This provision will lead to a lot of case law and may not be as simple as it might at first appear.

You must also bear in mind that the English and Welsh libel system is globally notorious as being a popular forum for claimants not living in the country but who are libelled online or by publication distributed in the UK and where they can show they have a legitimate reputation interest. The crude phrase used to describe this phenomenon is 'libel tourism'. A somewhat neutral way of looking at it would be to see the situation as choosing the best method to achieve redress for damage to reputation. EU treaty law means that Britain cannot follow the USA and introduce state and federal legislation to refuse to accept jurisdiction and enforce foreign court rulings – particularly in other EU member countries. However, the 2012 Defamation Bill through section 9 introduces the rule that:

> A court does not have jurisdiction to hear and determine an action by a person not domiciled in the UK, an EU Member State, or a state which is a contracting party to the Lugano Convention (Iceland, Norway, Denmark and Switzerland), unless the court is satisfied that, of all the places in which the statement complained of has been published, England and Wales is clearly the most appropriate place in which to bring an action in respect of the statement.

This appears to be a higher hurdle for foreign claimants e.g. showing there would be more than minimal damage caused by the publication in England, but again this is likely to be tested in future litigation.

★   A downloadable sound file defining and explaining libel. 3.2 Podcast downloadable https://soundcloud.com/ comparativemedialaw/podcast-3-2-uk-media-law

3.3   DEFENCES TO LIBEL

Your next step should be to find out if you may have any recognized defences, particularly if you think your copy is potentially defamatory.

You may be able to avoid getting sued if any of the following apply:

3.3.1   TRUTH/JUSTIFICATION

The story is true in substance and fact. In England and Wales the burden of proof is on the media defendant and not the claimant.

You need credible witnesses and evidence to persuade a jury on the balance of probabilities. This is expensive to defend. The current nature of the justification defence does not assist investigative journalism. The 2012 Defamation Bill has recommended the statutory definition of justification to be 'truth' with the need for:

> the defendant to show that the imputation conveyed by the statement complained of is substantially true. [...] If one or more of the imputations is not shown to be substantially true, the defence under this section does not fail if, having regard to the imputations which are shown to be substantially true, the imputations which are not shown to be substantially true do not seriously harm the claimant's reputation (section 2[1 and 3] of 2012 Defamation Bill).

✯ A downloadable sound file on truth/justification as a defence to libel.
3.31 Podcast downloadable https://soundcloud.com/comparativemedialaw/podcast-3-31-uk-media-law

3.3.2   ABSOLUTE PRIVILEGE/HIGH QUALIFIED PRIVILEGE

Absolute privilege. If your potentially defamatory material was said in open court – or in the Houses of Parliament – you should have absolute privilege/high qualified privilege. Court reporting if fair, accurate and contemporaneous (published to nearest deadline) will be absolutely privileged. The point about absolute privilege is that it is a defence to report libels expressed by people in court that they know to be untrue. Malice cannot undermine the defence of absolute privilege. This defence also applies to publications by Parliament and to parliamentarians when they make speeches during the proceedings of Parliament. The Defamation Bill 2012 proposes to extend absolute privilege to cover fair, accurate and contemporaneous reports of courts in any 'country or territory outside the United Kingdom'. This includes courts or tribunals established by international agreement or by the United Nations Security Council.

High qualified privilege. This defence applies to fair and accurate reports of past court hearings, and contemporary or past parliamentary proceedings. Only the malice of the reporter or publishing organization can undo this defence. This is a higher form of qualified privilege in the sense that media organizations are not obliged to publish in a suitable manner a reasonable letter or statement by way of explanation or contradiction from anyone claiming to have been defamed in the report. The adjectives 'high' and 'higher' are not used in the law or by lawyers, but applied by me to help distinguish the categories of qualified privilege. This high qualified privilege applies to: a fair and accurate report of proceedings in public of a legislature anywhere in the world; a fair and accurate report of proceedings in public before a court anywhere in the world (when not contemporaneous); a fair and accurate report of proceedings in public of a person appointed to hold a public inquiry by a government or legislature anywhere in the world; a fair and accurate report of proceedings in public anywhere in the world of an international organization or an international conference; a fair and accurate copy of or extract from any register or other document required by law to be open to public inspection; a notice or advertisement published by or on the authority of a court, or of a judge or officer of a court, anywhere in the world; a fair and accurate copy of or extract from matter published by or on the authority of a government or legislature anywhere in the world; a fair and accurate copy of or extract from matter published anywhere in the world by an international organization or an international conference (Schedule 1, Part 1 of the 1996 Defamation Act).

★   A downloadable sound file on the libel defence of absolute and high qualified privilege.
3.32 Podcast downloadable https://soundcloud.com/comparativemedialaw/podcast-3-32-uk-media-law

3.3.3   LOWER QUALIFIED PRIVILEGE

Qualified privilege subject to explanation or contradiction. I personally call this lower qualified privilege; the adjective 'lower' is not used in law, but applied by me to help with the classification and explanation of this area of libel law. If it was said at a public meeting (bona fide and lawfully held for a lawful purpose) – you should have qualified privilege subject to contradiction or explanation. The Defamation Bill 2012 is seeking to clarify that the meeting is held for the furtherance or discussion of a matter 'in the public interest' when the Defamation Act 1996 said it must be about a 'matter of public concern'. There would be merit in seeking the reply of anyone defamed at the meeting who was not there and could not put their side of the story. Indeed it would appear that BBC journalists are expected to do so. If the person(s) who believe they have been libelled contact you asking you to publish a report of their response you will only retain your qualified privilege by responding to their request within a reasonable period of time. All privileged reports seeking this defence have to be fair and accurate.

The Defamation Bill 2012 is intending to make statutory the common law impact of the *Turkington v Times* case of 2000, which provided a lower qualified privilege defence for press conferences: 'A fair and accurate report of proceedings at a press conference held anywhere in the world for the discussion of a matter of public interest.'

Turkington and Others v Times Newspapers Limited (Northern Ireland)
[2000] UKHL 57 (2nd November, 2000)
http://www.bailii.org/uk/cases/UKHL/2000/57.html

Press releases arising from the press conference should also be privileged though some caution should be exercised in using separate interviews recorded outside the conference which are unlikely to be covered.

Lower qualified privilege subject to contradiction or explanation also applies to statements made by senior police officers or government departments. It is useful to remember that firefighter, ambulance/paramedic, and coastguard bulletins are probably not privileged. It is worth repeating that 'subject to explanation or contradiction' means that if somebody accused of something wants to put their side of the story you should report it within a reasonable period of time. The Defamation Bill 2012 is intending to extend this category of qualified privilege to include fair and accurate reports of proceedings at meetings of any listed company in the world, and any public information issued by a legislature or government anywhere in the world; an authority anywhere in the world performing governmental functions; an international organization or international conference, and 'governmental functions' includes police functions. The privilege will also apply to a 'fair and accurate copy of, extract from or summary of a document made available by a court anywhere in the world, or by a judge or officer of such a court'.

It is as well to check what kind of meetings, associations and bodies carry higher and lower qualified privilege when reporting their events and statements, and the schedule is usually available online at: http://www.legislation.gov.uk/ukpga/1996/31/schedule/1. For example it is useful to be reminded that qualified privilege shields apply to associations 'formed for the purpose of promoting or encouraging the exercise of or interest in any art, science, religion or learning', 'for the purpose of promoting or safeguarding the interests of any trade, business, industry or profession', 'for the purpose of promoting or safeguarding the interests of a game, sport or pastime to the playing or exercise of which members of the public are invited or admitted', and 'for the purpose of promoting charitable objects or other objects beneficial to the community'.

✴   A downloadable sound file on the libel defence of qualified privilege subject to explanation or contradiction.
3.33 Podcast downloadable https://soundcloud.com/comparativemedialaw/podcast-3-33-the-uk-media-law

3.3.4   HONEST OPINION – PREVIOUSLY KNOWN AS FAIR COMMENT

If your report was a review or editorial, you might have a defence called 'honest opinion' (which used to be known as fair comment) but the comments must be honestly held opinions, based on true facts which are also a matter of public interest. Get all this right, then you might succeed.

a   It is clearly in the public interest to review a published novel, play, film, TV or radio programme, and the writings and utterances of published writers. The material has to be carefully examined to ensure that it fulfils all the criteria for the defence. The review needs to be written with honestly held opinions, free of malice, and all the comment has to be based on true facts.

b   The true facts would have to be justified on the balance of probabilities or on facts asserted in legally privileged arenas. The approach of the analysis has to be on a phrase-by-phrase, sentence-by-sentence basis. The true facts would have to be provable on the balance of probabilities with justification burden on the media defendant.

c   The construction of meaning in libel is based on the interpretation of readers in terms of 'ordinary and natural meaning'.

d   In a ruling of the Hong Kong Court of Final Appeal in 2000 (*Albert Cheng v Paul Tse*) Lord Nicholls indicated that nasty, vituperative comment should not be regarded as on the face malice. The fair comment/honest opinion defence should not be defeated when the writer is clearly actuated by spite, animosity, intent to injure, intent to arouse controversy or another motivation. He said: 'critics need no longer be mealy-mouthed in denouncing what they disagree with'.

> *Albert Cheng and Lam Yuk Wah v Tse Wai Chun Paul* [2000] HKCFA 35. Full ruling at:
> http://www.ipsofactoj.com/international/2000/Part7/int2000(7)–005.htm

e   You need to guard against imputations of improper motives. Lord Justice Bowen in 1885 said: 'The state of a man's mind is as much a matter of fact as the state of his digestion.' Personal comment about motive can easily become an assertion of a fact about human character.

f   While there is an argument that some phrases in reviews can be satirically surreal in the sense that nobody would believe the literal meaning inherent in the language, there is a difficulty that the 'bane' in these phrases is not removed by any antidote. It is possible that nowhere in an article can you find any clear and erasing communication that the phrases are metaphorical comedic nonsense. It would be possible to argue that the individuals identified would be loath to give the implied accusations the credibility of libel actions. It is also important to acknowledge that such sentences are attempts to describe the surreal and 'unbelievable' content.

g   In December 2010, the UK Supreme Court in the case of *Joseph v Spiller* ruled that: 'The defence of fair comment should be renamed "honest comment".' The Supreme Court declined to liberalize the defence, though they amended slightly one of the five steps defined by Lord Nicholls in *Tse Wai Chun Paul v Albert Cheng* 2000:

i   The comment had to be on a matter of public interest, which was not to be narrowly confined.

ii   It must be recognizable as comment, as distinct from an imputation of fact.

iii   It had to be based on facts which were true or protected by privilege.

iv   The comment had to be one which could have been made by an honest person, however prejudiced he might be, and however exaggerated or obstinate his views.

v   The Supreme Court adjusted one step to be explained as: 'The comment must, however, identify at least in general terms what it is that has led the commentator to make the comment, so that the reader can understand what the comment is about and the commentator can, if challenged, explain by giving particulars of the subject matter of his comment why he expressed the views that he did'.

Spiller & Anor v Joseph & Ors [2010] UKSC 53 (1 December 2010)
http://www.bailii.org/uk/cases/UKSC/2010/53.html

The 2012 Defamation Bill proposes in section 3 to codify this defence as 'honest opinion' and remove the public interest requirement so that the steps would be:

a   The statement complained of was a statement of opinion.
b   The statement complained of indicated, whether in general or specific terms, the basis of the opinion.
c   An honest person could have held the opinion on the basis of— (i) any fact which existed at the time the statement complained of was published; (ii) anything asserted to be a fact in a 'privileged statement' published before the statement complained of.
d   The defence will be defeated if the claimant shows that the defendant did not hold the opinion. (This does not apply when the defendant is quoting another person's opinion, though will apply if he/she knew or ought to have known that the author did not hold the opinion.)
e   The 'privileged statement' in (c) includes: responsible publication on matter of public interest, peer-reviewed statement in scientific or academic journal, reports of court proceedings protected by absolute privilege, and other reports protected by qualified privilege.

★   A downloadable sound file on the libel defence of honest opinion, previously known as fair comment.
3.34 Podcast downloadable https://soundcloud.com/comparativemedialaw/podcast-3-34-uk-media-law

3.3.5   RESPONSIBLE JOURNALISM

You might have a public interest privilege for responsible journalism that has mistakenly libelled somebody. The criteria for 'responsible journalism' include: giving fair opportunity for people criticized to give their side of the story, reporting a gist of this; evaluating reliability of your source, who might have an axe to grind; and avoiding sensationalist language and bias. The Jameel/Reynolds defence arises out of previous English House of Lords cases: *Albert Reynolds v Times Newspapers* 1999 and *Jameel v Wall Street Journal* 2006.

Reynolds v Times Newspapers Ltd and Ors [1999] UKHL 45; [1999] 4 All ER 609; [1999] 3 WLR 1010 (28th October, 1999)
http://www.bailii.org/uk/cases/UKHL/1999/45.html
Jameel & Ors v Wall Street Journal Europe Sprl [2006] UKHL 44 (11 October 2006)
http://www.bailii.org/uk/cases/UKHL/2006/44.html

In the first case Lord Nicholls set out a ten-point framework for responsible journalism, which could in certain circumstances mean that journalism produced in the public interest that had wrongly defamed individual(s) should not be liable for libel action.

Lord Nicholls's ten pointers for responsible journalism from *Reynolds v Times Newspapers* 1999:

1 The seriousness of the allegation. The more serious the charge, the more the public is misinformed and the individual harmed, if the allegation is not true.
2 The nature of the information, and the extent to which the subject matter is a matter of public concern.
3 The source of the information. Some informants have no direct knowledge of the events. Some have their own axes to grind, or are being paid for their stories.
4 The steps taken to verify the information.
5 The status of the information. The allegation may have already been the subject of an investigation which commands respect.
6 The urgency of the matter. News is often a perishable commodity.
7 Whether comment was sought from the plaintiff. He may have information others do not possess or have not disclosed. An approach to the plaintiff will not always be necessary.
8 Whether the article contained the gist of the plaintiff's side of the story.
9 The tone of the article. A newspaper can raise queries or call for an investigation. It need not adopt allegations as statements of fact.
10 The circumstances of the publication, including the timing.

In the second House of Lords case (*Jameel* 2006) the Law Lords decided the defence should turn on two issues: whether an article was on a matter of public interest and whether it was the product of responsible journalism. They said Lord Nicholls's ten factors should be useful pointers and not tests to be satisfied or hurdles to be jumped. As a result of the *Jameel* ruling, in 2007 investigative journalist Graeme McLagan, who had lost on a Reynolds libel defence over his book on police corruption *Bent Coppers* at the High Court, succeeded in his appeal.

Charman v Orion Group Publishing Group Ltd & Ors [2007] EWCA Civ 972 (10 October 2007)
http://www.bailii.org/ew/cases/EWCA/Civ/2007/972.html

The UK media has struggled to enjoy the benefits of clarity in relation to the responsible journalism defence because lower courts distinguish and interpret in different ways, and as the English legal system has more levels of appeal than most legal jurisdictions it can take years before final clarification, whether success or failure, is achieved at the highest level. This was the case in the dispute between Flood and *The Times*.

Flood v Times Newspapers Ltd [2012] UKSC 11 (21 March 2012)
http://www.bailii.org/uk/cases/UKSC/2012/11.html

Section 4 of the Defamation Bill 2012 at the time of writing proposed to codify and redefine this defence as: 'Responsible publication on matter of public interest'. The burden will be on the defence to show that 'the statement complained of was, or formed part of, a statement on a matter of public interest and the defendant acted responsibly in publishing the statement complained of'. The judges trying libel cases and deciding whether the responsible journalism defence applies 'may have regard' to nine criteria (amongst other matters) and these will replace the ten 'Reynolds defence criteria' set out by Lord Nicholls:

a   the nature of the publication and its context;

b   the seriousness of the imputation conveyed by the statement;

c   the relevance of the imputation conveyed by the statement to the matter of public interest concerned;

d   the importance of the matter of public interest concerned;

e   the information the defendant had before publishing the statement and what the defendant knew about the reliability of that information;

f   whether the defendant sought the claimant's views on the statement before publishing it and whether an account of any views the claimant expressed was published with the statement;

g   whether the defendant took any other steps to verify the truth of the imputation conveyed by the statement;

h   the timing of the statement's publication;

i   the tone of the statement.

While the Defamation Bill was being processed through Parliament, there was a political struggle over whether to replace section 4 with a more liberal and media-friendly public interest defence. Any changes to the Bill's content and evolution to Act of Parliament will be signposted on the companion website and by podcast. The Leveson Inquiry and its report raised the prospect of incentives for low-cost arbitration options in libel and privacy in the context of a post-PCC independent regulatory regime, whether backed by legislation or royal charter or not.

★   A downloadable sound file on the responsible journalism and public interest defence for libel.
3.35 Podcast downloadable https://soundcloud.com/comparativemedialaw/podcast-3-35-uk-media-law

3.3.6 NEUTRAL REPORTAGE

This was a developing common law defence arising out of the Reynolds defence of 1999 and was constructed by the Court of Appeal in *Al-Fagih v HH Saudi Research and Marketing* 2001 and Mr Justice Eady in *Roberts v Searchlight* in 2006.

Al-Fagih v HH Saudi Research & Marketing (UK) Ltd [2001] EWCA Civ
1634 (5 November 2001)
http://www.bailii.org/ew/cases/EWCA/Civ/2001/1634.html
Roberts & Anor v Gable & Ors [2006] EWHC 1025 (QB) (12 May 2006)
http://www.bailii.org/ew/cases/EWHC/QB/2006/1025.html

Under subsections 4(3) and 4(4) of the proposed Defamation Bill,
neutral reportage will be a statutory defence to libel 'where the
statement complained of was, or formed part of, an accurate and
impartial account of a dispute to which the claimant was a party'.
The defence also holds on the basis that 'when considering whether
the defendant acted responsibly, the court must disregard any omission by the defendant to take steps to verify the truth of the meaning
conveyed'. This defence is likely to succeed when the publication
fairly and accurately attributes and reports all sides to a dispute
that is defamatory and most importantly includes nothing by way of
headline, title, cue or content to suggest that the writer and publication is adopting or supporting defamatory allegations being made.

✶   A downloadable sound file on the neutral reportage defence
    to libel.
    3.36 Podcast downloadable https://soundcloud.com/
    comparativemedialaw/podcast-3-36-the-uk-media-law

3.3.7 INNOCENT DISSEMINATION

This is available for live broadcasters and Internet publishers and
is derived from section 1 of the 1996 Defamation Act. When a libel
comes out of the blue from a guest or participant in live programming you may have a defence particularly if you took reasonable
measures to prevent the publication and your live presenter(s) did
all that could be done to mitigate the sting of the libel when it was
uttered. The defence should also be available to Internet publishers
and service providers that do not have editorial control over their
content. It would be undermined if there was moderation or editing
of material before uploading and the online publisher and ISP
failed to take down or correct within a 'reasonable' period of time.

1996 Defamation Act http://www.legislation.gov.uk/ukpga/1996/31/contents

✶   A downloadable sound file on the libel defence of innocent dissemination.
3.37 Podcast downloadable https://soundcloud.com/comparativemedialaw/podcast-3-37-the-uk-media-law

3.3.8   PEER-REVIEWED STATEMENT IN SCIENTIFIC OR ACADEMIC JOURNAL AND AT CONFERENCE

Section 6 of the 2012 Defamation Bill proposed a special qualified privilege for 'publication of a statement in a scientific or academic journal'. To succeed the defendant (again the burden of proof, unlike in any other field of negligence, is on the defence) needs to meet the following conditions:

a   the statement relates to a scientific or academic matter;
b   before the statement was published in the journal an independent review of the statement's scientific or academic merit was carried out by the editor of the journal, and one or more persons with expertise in the scientific or academic matter concerned;
c   the privilege would be lost if the statement could be shown to have been made with malice;
d   the privilege also attaches to the assessment written by one or more of the persons who carried out the independent review of the statement.

The Defamation Bill 2012 also proposes to extend this category of lower qualified privilege to 'a fair and accurate report of proceedings of a scientific or academic conference held anywhere in the world, or copy of, extract from or summary of matter published by such a conference'.

✱   A downloadable sound file on the proposed libel defence for academics in published journals and at conferences.
3.38 Podcast downloadable https://soundcloud.com/comparativemedialaw/podcast-3-38-the-uk-media-law

3.3.9   WEBSITE OPERATOR DEFENCE

This is a new defence intended to be introduced by section 5 of the 2012 Defamation Bill and applies 'where an action for defamation is brought against the operator of a website in respect of a statement posted on the website'. It does not replace section 1 Innocent Dissemination in the 1996 Defamation Act. At first the defence would appear to be very simple in that: 'It is a defence for the operator to show that it was not the operator who posted the statement on the website.' But then the qualifications setting out how the defence would fail begin to complicate the situation: 'It was not possible for the claimant to identify the person who posted the statement, the claimant gave the operator a notice of complaint in relation to the statement, and the operator failed to respond to the notice of complaint in accordance with any provision contained in regulations.' The reference to 'regulations' promises a hornets' nest since these would be done by statutory instrument i.e. the government and the bill were very vague about the action a website operator would have to take 'relating to the identity or contact details of the person who posted the statement and action relating to its removal'.

Further to online libel issues, the proposal to introduce a single publication rule should remove the problem that every downloading of an Internet article amounts to a fresh publication with the statute of limitation on taking legal action being reactivated. In Britain any new downloading or viewing of a defamatory publication online represents a new libel. This 'problem' for the media was highlighted in the case of *Loutchansky v Times Newspapers* in its long and expensive route all the way to the ECtHR in 2009.

Times Newspapers Ltd (Nos 1 and 2) v The United Kingdom App no. 3002/03 [2009] ECtHR 451 (10 March 2009)
http://www.bailii.org/eu/cases/ECHR/2009/451.html

The peculiar jeopardy in English libel allowing further libel actions when the claimant can find a 'new publication' derives from the case of a German aristocrat, the Duke of Brunswick, who sent his butler in 1849 to London to buy an old back copy of a newspaper he had previously sued for libel, as the ECtHR President Lech Garlicki explained:

> On 19 September 1830 an article was published in the *Weekly Dispatch*. The limitation period for libel was, at that time, six years. The article defamed the Duke of Brunswick. Seventeen years after its publication an agent of the Duke purchased a back number containing the article from the *Weekly Dispatch*'s office. Another copy was obtained from the British Museum. The Duke sued on those two publications. The defendant contended that the cause of action was time-barred, relying on the original publication date. The court held that the delivery of a copy of the newspaper to the plaintiff's agent constituted a separate publication in respect of which suit could be brought.

The British media say these quaint anachronisms and narratives of history give the lack of freedom of expression and the claimant-friendly climate of UK media law a poor global reputation.

There are two important global media law issues relating to online libel that merit consideration. Putting a hyperlink to defamatory material on an online article is at the moment not in itself considered publication of the libellous material on another website that opens up in a separate frame or replaces the existing page. This was the unanimous decision of the Canadian Supreme Court in the 2011 case of *Wayne Crookes and West Coast Title Search Ltd v Jon Newton*.

Crookes v Newton, 2011 SCC 47 (CanLII), [2011] 3 SCR 269
http://canlii.ca/en/ca/scc/doc/2011/2011scc47/2011scc47.html

Hyperlinks are essentially references, which are fundamentally different from other acts of publication. To make hyperlinks a method of defamatory material reaching a third party would create liability for all those who used hyperlinks. This would have a seriously restrictive effect on the flow of information on the Internet and freedom of expression generally.

Defamatory material on the Internet can be sued over wherever it is downloaded. This appeared to be the implication of the 2002 Australian High Court decision in *Dow Jones & Co Inc v Gutnick* where it was ruled that a resident of the state of Victoria could sue an American publisher in the Victoria Supreme Court because the alleged libel could be downloaded on his terminal in Victoria. Justice Callinan said: 'If a publisher publishes in a multiplicity of jurisdictions it should understand, and must accept that it runs the risk of liability in those jurisdictions in which the publication is not lawful and it inflicts damage.'

Gutnick v Dow Jones & Co Inc [2001] VSC 305 (28 August 2001)
http://www.austlii.edu.au/cgi-bin/sinodisp/au/cases/vic/
VSC/2001/305.html
Dow Jones and Company Inc v Gutnick [2002] HCA 56; 210 CLR 575; 194 ALR 433; 77 ALJR 255 (10 December 2002)
http://www.austlii.edu.au/cgi-bin/sinodisp/au/cases/cth/
HCA/2002/56.html

As a final conclusion to this section on libel defences, I would urge you strongly to follow the rule if in doubt get professional legal advice before publication and without the substantial resources of an excellent in-house media legal department, I would always err on the side of caution.

★   A downloadable sound file on libel defences and issues for website publication.
3.39 Podcast downloadable https://soundcloud.com/comparativemedialaw/podcast-3-39-the-uk-media-law

3.4 PRIVACY – INTRODUCTION TO THE LEGAL CONCEPT

In the United Kingdom, journalists have to recognize a respect for the right to privacy under Article 8 of the Human Rights Act 1998 derived from the ECHR. This right is balanced with the right to freedom of expression set out in Article 10 and although the courts are supposed to have particular regard to freedom of expression they have to take into account the case law of the ECtHR at Strasbourg. The right to privacy means preventing the publication of true information that is private. It can also relate to private information that is untrue, but not libellous.

The English and European courts recognize that private information cannot be reported unless it is in the public interest. No-go areas include the nature of health treatment and state of health, education, sexuality, and personal relationships. It now means that people who do not give permission to be photographed in public and are not the subject of a public interest story are entitled to privacy protection. The principle of when media privacy law applies is when any individual has 'a reasonable expectation of privacy'. Privacy as a European legal concept means dignity, honour, reputation (overlapping with libel) identity, family life, home space, and private communications (correspondence, email, mobile, Skype, palm computer devices etc). It goes without saying that intercepting anyone's mobile, mail, email and communications devices is a criminal offence and so is giving bribes or impersonating anyone to unlawfully obtain private information. It is also a criminal offence and civil wrong to 'harass' anyone on the basis of causing distress on at least two separate occasions.

In Britain there has been rapid progress in establishing a media privacy law through the decisions of judges using Article 8 as the seed for their judicial activism. You need to know the exact text of Article 8 and its qualifying criteria. Privacy litigation is sometimes accompanied by arguments to override freedom of expression under Article 2 (right to life) and Article 3 (the right not to be tortured). This is leading to exceptional anonymity orders protecting notorious criminals in their new secret identities after release from custody from violent vigilante reprisals. In Northern Ireland the outweighing consideration of Articles 2 and 3 over Article 10 is leading judges to make anonymity orders on drug dealer defendants threatened with violence by paramilitary organizations. It is possible that a heightened consideration of Articles 2 and 3 could lead to this anonymity widening to more categories of convicted, sentenced and previously identified criminals or defendants on trial.

European Convention on Human Rights:

Article 2 – Right to life
Everyone's right to life shall be protected by law. No one shall be deprived of his life intentionally save in the execution of a sentence of a court following his conviction of a crime for which this penalty is provided by law.

Article 3 – Prohibition of torture
No one shall be subjected to torture or to inhuman or degrading treatment or punishment.

Privacy versus freedom of expression:

Article 8 – Privacy
1   Everyone has the right to respect for his private and family life, his home and his correspondence.
2   There shall be no interference by a public authority with the exercise of this right except such as is in accordance with the law and is necessary in a democratic society in the interests of national security, public safety or the economic well-being of the country, for the prevention of disorder or crime, for the protection of health or morals, or for the protection of the rights and freedoms of others.

Article 10 – Freedom of expression
1   Everyone has the right to freedom of expression. This right shall include freedom to hold opinions and to receive and impart information and ideas without interference by public authority and regardless of frontiers. This article shall not prevent States from requiring the licensing of broadcasting, television or cinema enterprises.
2   The exercise of these freedoms, since it carries with it duties and responsibilities, may be subject to such formalities, conditions, restrictions or penalties as are prescribed by law and are

necessary in a democratic society, in the interests of national security, territorial integrity or public safety, for the prevention of disorder or crime, for the protection of health or morals, for the protection of the reputation or rights of others, for preventing the disclosure of information received in confidence, or for maintaining the authority and impartiality of the judiciary.

All the articles from the convention as enshrined in Schedule 1 HRA 1998 are available at:
http://www.legislation.gov.uk/ukpga/1998/42/schedule/1</

✳ A downloadable sound file explaining the media respect for the right to privacy and other competing human rights. 3.4 Podcast downloadable https://soundcloud.com/comparativemedialaw/podcast-3-4-the-uk-media-law

3.5 DEVELOPMENT OF UK MEDIA PRIVACY LAW

In 2004 a slim majority of Law Lords in Britain's highest court of the time (The Judicial Committee of the House of Lords) affirmed a right to privacy for the model Naomi Campbell in a news article published in the *Daily Mirror* newspaper. Campbell had lied to the general public when she denied taking drugs. The *Mirror* published a photograph of her proving the lie. But Ms Campbell said her privacy had been invaded because she was photographed leaving a Narcotics Anonymous meeting in the affluent Chelsea area of London. The *Daily Mirror* newspaper said the photograph was taken in a public street and there was a public interest in publishing it. The Law Lords' decision was by a majority of three to two and it was argued that this weakened the importance of freedom of expression when investigating the alleged hypocrisy of public figures. The majority of the Law Lords emphasized that the privacy being protected related to Ms Campbell's medical treatment for addiction. There would not have been a problem with the publication of the photograph had it not been linked to the revelation she was undergoing medical treatment for addiction illness.

> *Campbell v MGN Ltd* [2004] UKHL 22 (6 May 2004)
> http://www.bailii.org/uk/cases/UKHL/2004/22.html

In the same year Princess Caroline of Monaco won a case at the European Court of Human Rights on the basis that taking her picture with her children while in a public place was an invasion of her privacy. The tabloid media argued that the law gave a privilege of privacy to a wealthy international celebrity and member of a European royal family.

> *Von Hannover v Germany* App no. 59320/00 [2004] ECtHR 294 (24 June 2004)
> http://www.bailii.org/eu/cases/ECHR/2004/294.html

There then followed a legal struggle over the boundary of privacy law in taking photographs of public figures on private business in public places. In 2007 the successful author J.K. Rowling was initially unsuccessful in a privacy action against photographs taken of her with her partner and children in Edinburgh. But she did win on appeal.

> *Murray v Big Pictures (UK) Ltd* [2008] EWCA Civ 446 (07 May 2008)
> http://www.bailii.org/ew/cases/EWCA/Civ/2008/446.html

There have been developments in legal privacy issues that went beyond the concerns of media celebrity. Initially the British legal system would not create a tort of privacy for Mrs Mary Wainwright from Leeds and her son, who had learning difficulties and had been strip-searched when visiting her other son in prison. The Law Lords ruled that there was no privacy law in Britain and it was a matter for Parliament to enact one. But in September 2006 the ECtHR ruled that Mrs Wainwright and her son had experienced a violation of ECHR Article 8 (right to respect for private and family life) and Article 13 (right to an effective remedy.) It could be argued that the Strasbourg Court ruling is powerful precedent that should be taken into account by the UK courts in recognizing a more general tort of privacy through the Article 8 concept.

> *Wainwright v The United Kingdom* App no. 12350/04 [2006] ECtHR 807 (26 September 2006)
> http://www.bailii.org/eu/cases/ECHR/2006/807.html

The developing privacy cases underlined the fact that Article 10 freedom of expression was not a trump card and did not have greater importance than Article 8 privacy. The two rights had to be 'balanced' by judges in an intense investigation of the facts of each case on its merits and section 12 of the HRA said the courts would have to refer to the ethical and regulatory journalism codes such as those published by the PCC, BBC and Ofcom. Even though the legislation said the courts had to have 'particular regard' to Article 10, this was not interpreted as being a statutory obligation to give freedom of expression priority or greater importance than any other right in the Act and Convention.

Some national newspaper editors such as Paul Dacre of the *Daily Mail* complained that this had been a back-door route to developing detailed privacy law without the due process of parliamentary legislation.

> Paul Dacre's speech on privacy to the Society of Editors in 2008 criticizing the development of 'back-door privacy law'
> http://www.societyofeditors.co.uk/page-view.
> php?pagename=thesoelecture2008

The death of Diana, Princess of Wales in 1997 and the controversial issue of paparazzi culpability in that event would also appear to have influenced European legal culture about the need to protect celebrity and public figures from an accumulating harassment in public and private that undermines a sense of personal dignity and privacy. The courts were heavily guided by the privacy provisions in the regulatory codes issued by the PCC, BBC and Ofcom when evaluating what was considered a reasonable or legitimate expectation of privacy and whether there was public interest in publication. Many of the decisions were made in confidential private hearings, described by the media as 'secret' when considering injunctions that prevented broadcasts or print publications occurring. These are known as 'prior restraints' in law and the practice became controversial when added injunctions banning publication of the existence of the original injunctions were issued. These were called 'super-injunctions'. Many lawyers and judges in the UK began to concede that there was a clear and developing media law of a respect to the right of privacy, though it would not be classified as a separate and free-standing general civil wrong 'tort' of privacy.

The trend was confirmed in December 2006 with two Appeal Court rulings. In *Loreena McKennitt v Ash* the judges supported the High Court judge Mr Justice Eady who ruled that a book by McKennitt's former friend, *Travels with Loreena McKennitt: My Life as a Friend*, revealed personal and private detail that the singer was entitled to keep secret.

Ash & Anor v McKennitt & Ors [2006] EWCA Civ 1714 (14 December 2006)
http://www.bailii.org/ew/cases/EWCA/Civ/2006/1714.html

In *HRH Prince of Wales v Associated Newspapers*, the Court of Appeal decided the *Daily Mail* was not entitled to publish substantial extracts from a handwritten journal kept by Prince Charles relating to his visit to Hong Kong in 1993 when the colony was handed over to China. In a balancing exercise the judges decided that it was necessary to restrict freedom of expression in order to prevent disclosure of information received in confidence. The court had to decide whether it was in the public interest that the duty of confidence should be breached. The McKennitt precedent stood after no appeal was pursued at the House of Lords.

Associated Newspapers Ltd v HRH Prince of Wales [2006] EWCA Civ 1776 (21 December 2006)
http://www.bailii.org/ew/cases/EWCA/Civ/2006/1776.html

Rulings by Mr Justice Eady in 2007 and 2008 emphasized the shift in the application of the balance between privacy and freedom of expression. In *T v BBC* he ruled that an interview with an adult mother with learning difficulties and film of her being separated from her child because social workers had judged the child to be at risk could not be broadcast even though the woman and her social worker had consented.

T v The British Broadcasting Corporation (BBC) [2007] EWHC 1683 (QB) (11 July 2007)
http://www.bailii.org/ew/cases/EWHC/QB/2007/1683.html

In *Mosley v News Group Newspapers*, he decided that surreptitious filming of Max Mosley's S & M activities with women wearing uniforms and applying prison-style punishment techniques was not in the public interest and awarded Mr Mosley £60,000 in damages.

Mosley v News Group Newspapers Ltd [2008] EWHC 1777 (QB) (24 July 2008)
http://www.bailii.org/ew/cases/EWHC/QB/2008/1777.html

In Grand Chamber rulings on two cases from Germany in February 2011 (Caroline of Hanover and Axel Springer) the ECtHR judges ruled that the balance should be in favour of freedom of expression (Article 10) in relation to the photographing of Princess Caroline of Monaco in public when there was interest in the illness of her father, and the identification of a well-known television actor, famous for his role as a police superintendent, for being arrested and convicted of possessing cocaine. The court stated: 'the public's right to be informed can even extend to aspects of the private life of public figures, particularly where politicians are concerned'. But 'this will not be the case – even where the persons concerned are quite well known to the public – where the published photos and accompanying commentaries relate exclusively to details of the person's private life and have the sole aim of satisfying the curiosity of a particular readership in that respect'.

> *Von Hannover v Germany (no. 2)* App no. 40660/08 [2012] ECtHR 228 (7 February 2012)
> http://www.bailii.org/eu/cases/ECHR/2012/228.html
> *Axel Springer AG v Germany* App no. 39954/08 [2012] ECtHR 227 (7 February 2012)
> http://www.bailii.org/eu/cases/ECHR/2012/227.html

In 2011 the granting of privacy injunctions and super-injunctions (banning the reporting of the existence of an injunction itself) in relation to the private lives of celebrities became controversial when thousands of Twitter users defied an injunction relating to the private life of Manchester United player Ryan Giggs. There was also disquiet over the existence of an injunction granted in a private hearing in relation to the multinational company Trafigura and its disposal of waste chemicals. High Court rulings in 2011 did not grant injunctions against the media in respect of the private lives of premiership soccer players John Terry and Rio Ferdinand and Parliament asked a senior judge to report on the practice and justification of using prior restraint and 'super-injunctions' as a remedy for Article 8 litigation. It might be a fair argument to say that the dispute over prior restraint on private lives privacy is ongoing and it seems that almost week by week a popular newspaper might claim a victory for press freedom in resisting an injunction only for another injunction to be granted with the anodyne reference to initials as a representation of the person protected. What is not in dispute is that the struggle involves high legal costs for the media and people seeking protection. In the autumn of 2012 the media succeeded in resisting a prior restraint injunction in the case of the private life of a former England soccer manager.

> *McClaren v News Group Newspapers Ltd* [2012] EWHC 2466 (QB) (05 September 2012)
> http://www.bailii.org/ew/cases/EWHC/QB/2012/2466.html

A month later, an injunction obtained by a celebrity comedian to keep his name out of the coverage of the scandal relating to the deceased BBC disc jockey Jimmy Savile was successfully overturned:

'Media wins court battle to overturn injunction'
http://www.guardian.co.uk/uk/2012/oct/04/freddie-starr-itv-injunction
Findings of a committee chaired by the Master of the Rolls, Lord
Neuberger, on super-injunctions, anonymity injunctions and open
justice, May 2011
http://www.judiciary.gov.uk/Resources/JCO/Documents/Reports/
super-injunction-report–20052011.pdf
Super-injunctions press conference transcript
http://www.judiciary.gov.uk/media/media-releases/2011/Superinjuncti
ons+press+conference+transcript.htm
'Super-injunctions, gagging orders and injunctions: the full list.
Guardian research shows newspapers are quick to drop public interest
arguments for stories about celebrities'
http://www.guardian.co.uk/law/datablog/2011/aug/05/
superinjunctions-gagging-orders-injunctions-list<

✱   A downloadable sound file on the development of media
     privacy law in the UK.
     3.5 Podcast downloadable https://soundcloud.com/
     comparativemedialaw/podcast-3-5-the-uk-media-law

3.6 PRIVACY BY MEDIA REGULATION (SECONDARY MEDIA LAW)

Section 3 of the PCC Editors' Code of Practice is clearly based on Article 8 of the ECHR:

i   Everyone is entitled to respect for his or her private and family life, home, health and correspondence, including digital communications.
ii   Editors will be expected to justify intrusions into any individual's private life without consent. Account will be taken of the complainant's own public disclosures of information.

iii It is unacceptable to photograph individuals in private places without their consent.

Note – Private places are public or private property where there is a reasonable expectation of privacy.

UK broadcasters had been under a statutory obligation to respect privacy before the 1998 HRA came into force in October 2000 because sections 107(1) and 130 of the Broadcasting Act 1996 required Ofcom to consider complaints about unwarranted infringement of privacy in a programme or in connection with the obtaining of material included in a programme. Broadcasting regulation was continued and extended by sections 3(2)(f) and 326 of the Communications Act 2003. The obligations are clearly stated and then given explanation in Ofcom's published 'Broadcasting Code' and the BBC's 'Editorial Guidelines': 'Any infringement of privacy in programmes, or in connection with obtaining material included in programmes, must be warranted.' Sections 8.2 to 8.22 define the best practices to be followed when gathering material for broadcasting and then transmitting it in terms of 'private lives' and 'public places' and for some reason broadcasting law uses the adjective 'legitimate' instead of 'reasonable' in relation to the expectation of privacy involved.

BBC Editorial Guidelines Section 7 on Privacy
http://www.bbc.co.uk/editorialguidelines/page/guidelines-privacy-introduction/
Ofcom Broadcasting Code Section 8 on Privacy
http://stakeholders.ofcom.org.uk/broadcasting/broadcast-codes/broadcast-code/privacy/

In all three professional fields it is recognized that privacy is not an absolute right and can be compromised in the public interest, and *The Editors' Codebook* by Ian Beales argues that 'privacy is not a commodity which can be sold on one person's terms – the Code is not designed to protect commercial deals' – perhaps something of a swipe at some judicial decisions that have been accused of doing just that.

How does the balancing process work in practice? The BBC in its detailed and comprehensive guides divides practices in terms of privacy and consent and focusing on the impact of conduct and publication on children and vulnerable people, third parties, and using material from social media (http://www.bbc.co.uk/editorialguidelines/page/guidelines-privacy-privacy-consent/), secretrecording(http://www.bbc.co.uk/editorialguidelines/page/guidelines-privacy-practices-secret-recording/), webcams (http://www.bbc.co.uk/editorialguidelines/page/guidelines-privacy-practices-webcams/), doorstepping (http://www.bbc.co.uk/editorialguidelines/page/guidelines-privacy-doorstepping/), tag-along raids with police and state investigators (http://www.bbc.co.uk/editorialguidelines/page/guidelines-privacy-tag-along/), reporting death, suffering and distress (http://www.bbc.co.uk/editorialguidelines/page/guidelines-privacy-death-suffering-distress/), and handling personal information in terms of contributors' details, cookies, sending emails, viral marketing and missing people (http://www.bbc.co.uk/editorialguidelines/page/guidelines-privacy-personal-information/).

I suppose useful amber lights over potential problems are signposted by the BBC's very long list of 'mandatory referrals' to the Director Editorial Policy and Standards, supervisory editors and commissioning editors, which includes anything from a proposal to carry out secret recording to any proposal to doorstep, whether in person or on the phone, for comedy and entertainment purposes (Mandatory referrals Privacy http://www.bbc.co.uk/editorialguidelines/page/guidelines-privacy-mandatory-referrals/).

✶　A downloadable sound file on privacy by secondary media law and regulation.
3.6 Podcast downloadable https://soundcloud.com/comparativemedialaw/podcast-3-6-the-uk-media-law

3.7 RECOGNIZING THE BOUNDARIES IN PRIVACY

The PCC has recognized that a large majority of social media users would not be happy for the information they publish to be used in mainstream media, and journalists are advised to justify the use of personal information from Internet sources. A ruling of the PCC in 2012 justified the use by the media of publicly available content posted on Facebook, though it was not asked to deal with the issue of copyright in relation to photographs or images.

> PCC rules on privacy complaint about local newspaper story that used information from Facebook
> http://www.pcc.org.uk/news/index.html?article=ODEzNQ
> Press Complaints Commission Guidance Note: Privacy and the public Domain in the age of social media
> http://www.pcc.org.uk/advice/editorials-detail.html?article=ODEwNw

Details of the home addresses of public figures need to be considered in terms of security issues and the threat of stalkers. Health issues are obviously an area 'generally protected under the Code' and the PCC has recognized that speculation about pregnancy can be intrusive before an individual has had the wish or the chance to inform family or friends. Most PCC adjudications concern the rights and wrongs of balancing decisions between privacy, public interest and media publication interest in relation to the famous, infamous, public servants and members of the Royal Family. In respect of photographs, the PCC has asked media editors to ask the questions: was the person photographed out of the public view – not visible or identifiable with the naked eye to someone in a public place and was he or she engaged in a private activity at the time? Public interest is explored in more detail in the next chapter, but editors are urged to genuinely apply the public interest test and evaluate whether the 'degree of intrusion is proportionate to the public interest served'. Using material gained from a police raid when the homeowner denied any knowledge of the offence alleged and was not charged would not be considered acceptable. Using secret photography or filming of a public figure/celebrity when doing something that was neither a crime, improper, nor antisocial would not serve any public interest. It was generally accepted that intimate photographs of the Duchess of Cambridge published in magazines in France and Italy would have breached the PCC

Editors' Code and UK media respect for the right of privacy since she had a reasonable expectation of privacy, which was not over-ridden by any public interest.

Boundaries have been set in PCC 'jurisprudence' in relation to conduct and publication that amounts to 'gratuitous humilia-tion', and guidance on the coverage of lottery winners serves as a useful 'common-sense' application of privacy ethics. Subject to strong public interest justification, the decision of winners to opt for anonymity should generally be respected, whatever the scale of their jackpot; winners who opt for publicity are still protected from publication of inaccurate information and harassment, and mate-rial they had not put into the public domain; very young, old, sick or recently bereaved winners who could be classed as 'vulnerable' should be accorded 'strong protection under the code'; and offering rewards and inducements to anyone to identify anonymous lottery winners is banned. In summary, the PCC has recognized a seven-step approach to judging the privacy balance: is consent for publi-cation explicitly given or implied; has the subject compromised his or her right to privacy by courting publicity and commodifying their private life 'on their own terms'; is the subject a public figure or role model and does the publication reflect on their public or professional status or image; is the information already in the public domain and would it 'be reasonable for it to be retrieved and made private'; have people who have been photographed without their consent any reasonable expectation of privacy in terms of being out of public view and 'engaged in private activity'; is the publication in the public interest; and is the breach of privacy proportionate to the public interest served?

Some illustrative case histories: In 2008 BBC Radio 2 comedy artists Russell Brand and Jonathan Ross made 'prank calls' to the actor and writer Andrew Sachs about his granddaughter who performed in a pop group. This was investigated as a breach of privacy and harm and offence by both the BBC and Ofcom who had dual regulatory jurisdiction. The Ofcom Sanctions Committee fined the BBC a total of £150,000 and observed that the material aired had 'a cumulative effect which resulted in it overall being exceptionally offensive, humiliating and demeaning'.

http://stakeholders.ofcom.org.uk/binaries/enforcement/content-sanctions-adjudications/BBCRadio2TheRussellBrandShow.pdf
The BBC Trust had apologized for the programming and condemned the behaviour of the artists, and the editorial decision-making that approved the broadcasts:
Editorial Standards Findings: Appeals and editorial issues considered by the Trust's Editorial Standards Committee in Russell Brand et al and Radio 2 and Radio 1 October 2008
http://news.bbc.co.uk/nol/shared/bsp/hi/pdfs/21_11_08_brand_ross_moyles.pdf
BBC News page 'Timeline: Russell Brand prank calls'
http://news.bbc.co.uk/1/hi/entertainment/7694989.stm
PCC ruling on unjustifiable use of video derived from a police raid.
Popple v *Scarborough Evening News*: report 77, 2008
http://www.pcc.org.uk/news/index.html?article=NTE0OQ
PCC ruling on unjustifiable use of photographs taken without the consent of a supermodel with her family on holiday abroad.
Macpherson v *Hello!*: Report 74, 2007
http://www.pcc.org.uk/news/index.html?article=NDMyMA
PCC ruling on gratuitous humiliation in relation to a *News of the World* article that included an excess of intimate detail. A woman v *News of the World*: Report 74, 2007
http://www.pcc.org.uk/news/index.html?article=NDMzMQ
PCC ruling on a 'fishing expedition' by *Daily Telegraph* reporters who posed as constituents to talk to Liberal Democrat ministers at their constituency surgeries. Liberal Democrat Party v *Daily Telegraph* Report, May 2011
http://www.pcc.org.uk/news/index.html?article=NzEyMA

In 2012 the potential tragic consequences of not obtaining the consent of people unwittingly subject to media pranks were amplified when a nurse who had been duped in a call by two Australian radio presenters subsequently died. She had been working at the private hospital in London where the Duchess of Cambridge was being treated for her pregnancy condition. Ofcom requires broadcasters to inform interviewees that they are being recorded for broadcast or taking part in a live transmission. People subject to stunt or prank interaction should usually be pre-recorded and their consent obtained prior to publication.

⋆   A downloadable sound file on recognizing the ethical
     boundaries in media privacy.
     3.7 Podcast downloadable https://soundcloud.com/
     comparativemedialaw/podcast-3-7-the-uk-media-law

3.8   INACCURATE PUBLICATION – NEITHER LIBELLOUS NOR BREACH OF PRIVACY, BROADCASTING IMPARTIALITY AND 'UNDUE PROMINENCE OF VIEWS AND OPINIONS'

Media regulation in the UK places a high professional responsibility on journalists to be accurate and promptly and with 'due prominence' to correct their errors with apologies where appropriate. It is the first rule of the Editors' code:

i   The Press must take care not to publish inaccurate, misleading
     or distorted information, including pictures.
ii   A significant inaccuracy, misleading statement or distortion
     once recognised must be corrected, promptly and with due
     prominence, and – where appropriate – an apology published.
     In cases involving the Commission, prominence should be
     agreed with the PCC in advance.

Furthermore, the PCC expected publications to fairly and accurately report the outcome of libel actions. However, the 2012 Defamation Bill under section 12 proposes to give courts the power to order a summary of their judgments to be published by the media defendant. There is no public interest exception to account for inaccuracy. Editors need to show reasonable grounds for believing the stories they publish are accurate, that proper checks have been made and when mistakes happen, giving an 'adequate opportunity to respond' to allegations is encouraged though not mandatory. In fact under the heading 'Opportunity to reply', section 2 of the Editors' Code of Practice explicitly states: 'A fair opportunity for reply to inaccuracies must be given when reasonably called for.' For example, stories based on a single anonymous source would appear to require a response from the other side. The PCC has upheld complaints about factual distortion:

> Ms Alicia SIngh v *Closer*: Report 79, 2009
> http://www.pcc.org.uk/news/index.html?article=NTc3MA
> It has upheld complaints when the subject of a story had not been offered a prompt and proportionate chance to reply following publication:
> Mr Paul Burrell v *News of the World*: Report 78, 2008
> http://www.pcc.org.uk/news/index.html?article=NTQwNQ

The PCC did not recognize a mandatory right of reply – something being campaigned for in the context of the 'Hackgate' scandal and Leveson Inquiry – but it does support consideration of providing the opportunity in terms of the merits and circumstances of the story. It has also issued special guidance bulletins to improve the standard of accuracy during journalism campaigns on the reporting of cases involving paedophiles (http://www.pcc.org.uk/news/index.html?article=OTQ=), and the reporting of mental health issues (http://www.pcc.org.uk/news/index.html?article=NDE5OQ). To counter any perceived misrepresentation of 'refugees and asylum seekers', news coverage is measured against objective correlatives defining an asylum seeker as 'a person currently seeking refugee status or humanitarian protection', a refugee for example 'as someone who has fled their country in fear of their life' and an 'illegal immigrant as being a person who had been refused such status and had failed to respond to a removal notice to quit Britain'.

> Harman and Harman v *Folkestone Herald*: Report 47, 1999
> http://www.pcc.org.uk/news/index.html?article=MTgzOQ

The post-Leveson press industry regulatory system is expected to be more independent of influence by newspaper editors. The Leveson Inquiry Report summarized an agreed strategy of giving it the power to impose fines of up to £1 million or less than 1% of turnover, order prominent published corrections, and/or apologies. Pro-active investigations, a conscience clause in journalists' contracts, whistle-blowing hotline, and accepting third-party complaints (as received by Ofcom) were also on the agenda.

Under section 5 of the Ofcom Broadcast Code news broadcasters in the UK are under greater regulatory duty to ensure reporting is done 'with due accuracy and presented with due impartiality'.

Significant mistakes should normally be acknowledged and corrected on air quickly. Corrections should be appropriately scheduled. In addition no politician may be used as a newsreader, interviewer or reporter in any news programmes unless, 'exceptionally, it is editorially justified'.

Ofcom – Section Five: Due Impartiality and Due Accuracy and Undue Prominence of Views and Opinions
http://stakeholders.ofcom.org.uk/broadcasting/broadcast-codes/broadcast-code/impartiality/

In those circumstances the political allegiance of that person must be made clear to the audience. Broadcasters have a duty to avoid giving 'undue prominence of views and opinions', and in practice this means that presenters and programmes are obliged to 'put the other side' or represent a balance and reply in argument and dispute. When a programme or sequence is heavily or wholly slanted to one political view or opinion, the broadcaster is obliged by regulation to ensure that the spectrum of argument is balanced perhaps by a programme arguing the opposite or the opportunity for political opponents to have similar representation, time and presence in the programming. The BBC recognizes that the Ofcom Code obliges them to seek a response from individuals or organizations who are the subject of significant criticism or allegations of wrongdoing or incompetence (http://www.bbc.co.uk/editorialguidelines/page/guidance-right-reply-full).

This legal duty in compliance is not imposed on print, magazine and online journalists who are 'free to be partisan' though section 1(iii) of the Editors' Code does state that the press 'must distinguish clearly between comment, conjecture and fact'.

Claims should not be presented as fact: A.J. Crompton v *The Sun*: Report 41, 1997
http://www.pcc.org.uk/news/index.html?article=MTk4MQ
In its first criticism of an online blogger, the PCC declared opinion should not be presented as fact with the onus on a magazine to 'correct authoritatively':
Mr Oli Bird v *The Spectator*: 2010
http://www.pcc.org.uk/news/index.html?article=NjMxNg

The BBC Editorial Guidelines state that it is committed to 'achieving due accuracy' and recognizes that accuracy is 'also a requirement under the Agreement accompanying the BBC Charter' (http://www.bbc.co.uk/editorialguidelines/page/guidelines-accuracy-introduction/). The BBC provides best practice guidelines in the seven categories of gathering material (http://www.bbc.co.uk/editorialguidelines/page/guidelines-accuracy-gathering-material/) to correcting mistakes (http://www.bbc.co.uk/editorialguidelines/page/guidelines-accuracy-correcting-mistakes/). The professional expectation is that its journalists should gather material using first-hand sources wherever possible, check and cross-check facts, validate the authenticity of documentary evidence and digital material, corroborate claims and allegations made by contributors wherever possible, and that it should always be remembered that in news and current affairs, 'achieving accuracy is more important than speed'. The BBC's Editorial Guidelines are also very detailed on the subject of 'due impartiality'– another obligation in the charter agreement in relation to 'matters of public policy or political or industrial controversy' (http://www.bbc.co.uk/editorialguidelines/page/guidelines-impartiality-introduction/). The BBC provides staff guides on nine areas from 'breadth and diversity of opinion' (http://www.bbc.co.uk/editorialguidelines/page/guidelines-impartiality-breadth-diversity-opinion/) to 'personal view content' (http://www.bbc.co.uk/editorialguidelines/page/guidelines-impartiality-personal-view/). As an emergency first stop if you are working for the BBC I would always check the mandatory referral pages which in this section relate to accuracy (http://www.bbc.co.uk/editorialguidelines/page/guidelines-accuracy-mandatory-referrals/)

and impartiality (http://www.bbc.co.uk/editorialguidelines/page/
guidelines-impartiality-mandatory-referrals/).

Statutory broadcast regulation can fine in terms of millions
of pounds and delete the licence of a broadcaster altogether.
Somewhat dramatic examples include a fine of £2 million
imposed on Carlton Television by the former Independent
Television Commission in 1998 following the *Guardian* newspaper's revelation that dramatized sequences had been represented
as documentary journalism, and Press TV, which had its licence
revoked in January 2012 when it emerged that editorial control of
the channel rested with Press TV International based in Tehran.
Press TV had refused to pay a fine of £100,000 over the recording
and transmission of an interview obtained under duress from the
Newsweek and Channel 4 journalist Maziar Bahari while in an
Iranian prison.

Press TV licence revoked 20 January 2012
http://stakeholders.ofcom.org.uk/binaries/enforcement/broadcast-
licence-conditions/press-tv-revocation.pdf

✸   A downloadable sound file on the secondary media law
relating to balance and accuracy.
3.8 Podcast downloadable https://soundcloud.com/
comparativemedialaw/podcast-3-8-the-uk-media-law

3.9 UNFAIR PUBLICATION AND/OR CAUSING HARM AND OFFENCE

There is no primary media law making it a civil wrong or criminal offence to publish 'unfairly' though it might be argued that a
subjective construction of 'harm' and 'offence' is part of the law of
libel and privacy. But unfairness and 'harm and offence' are key
issues in secondary media law and this means consequential harm
and offence beyond criminal and civil law are professional ethical
issues of enormous importance.

The BBC's Editorial Guidelines have an entire category (section 5) devoted to harm and offence and again it is essential that any BBC employee, whether staff, freelance or independent contractor, is fully aware of the mandatory referrals (http://www.bbc.co.uk/editorialguidelines/page/guidelines-harm-mandatory-referrals/).

The BBC Radio Russell Brand and Jonathan Ross affair of 2008 is highly illustrative of when regulators recognize harm and offence and the Corporation's guidelines have detailed briefings on anything from 'intimidation and humiliation' (http://www.bbc.co.uk/editorialguidelines/page/guidelines-harm-intimida-tion/) to the reporting of tragic events (http://www.bbc.co.uk/editorialguidelines/page/guidelines-harm-tragic-events/).

The boundaries can be seen as culturally specific to the UK. For example what might be considered acceptable in terms of aggressive and conviction-style talk presentation in the USA is regarded as unacceptable in Britain as Ofcom would rule on the conduct of an interview by Jon Gaunt on TalkSport in 2008.

Ofcom Broadcast Bulletin Issue number 133–11 May 2009, In Breach Jon Gaunt Talksport, 7 November 2008, 11:25
http://stakeholders.ofcom.org.uk/binaries/enforcement/broadcast-bulletins/obb133/issue133.pdf
Mr Gaunt lost his contract, the radio station was publicly 'reprimanded' and his attempt to seek redress in the courts on the basis of freedom of expression, with the support of the civil rights organization Liberty, were unsuccessful at the High Court
Gaunt v OFCOM [2010] EWHC 1756 (QB) (13 July 2010)
http://www.bailii.org/cgi-bin/markup.cgi?doc=/ew/cases/EWHC/QB/2010/1756.html
and the Appeal Court in 2011
Gaunt, R (on the application of) v The Office of Communications [2011] EWCA Civ 692 (17 June 2011)
http://www.bailii.org/cgi-bin/markup.cgi?doc=/ew/cases/EWCA/Civ/2011/692.html

---

Section 2 of the Ofcom Broadcasting Code places a statutory obligation on UK broadcasters to recognize that:

2.1 Generally accepted standards must be applied to the contents of television and radio services so as to provide adequate protection for members of the public from the inclusion in such services of harmful and/or offensive material.

2.2 Factual programmes or items or portrayals of factual matters must not materially mislead the audience.

2.3 In applying generally accepted standards broadcasters must ensure that material which may cause offence is justified by the context (see meaning of 'context' below). Such material may include, but is not limited to, offensive language, violence, sex, sexual violence, humiliation, distress, violation of human dignity, discriminatory treatment or language (for example on the grounds of age, disability, gender, race, religion, beliefs and sexual orientation). Appropriate information should also be broadcast where it would assist in avoiding or minimizing offence.

Ofcom and the BBC coincide with caution and protocols on the representation of violence, suicide, nudity, sex, hypnosis, the occult, paranormal and life-changing advice. Ofcom places an obligation on all broadcasting under section 7 of its code that all licensees 'must avoid unjust or unfair treatment of individuals or organisations in programmes'.

Section 7 of the Ofcom Broadcasting Code
http://stakeholders.ofcom.org.uk/broadcasting/broadcast-codes/broadcast-code/fairness/
The BBC Editorial Guidelines set out an extensive range of rules and guidance on 'fairness, contributors and consent'
http://www.bbc.co.uk/editorialguidelines/page/guidelines-fairness-introduction/
with a clear briefing on mandatory referrals
http://www.bbc.co.uk/editorialguidelines/page/guidelines-fairness-mandatoryreferrals/
Ofcom has from time to time published special briefings and guidance on its code. After adjudicating on a number of complaints about extreme language used on the radio, it released 'Offensive Language on the Radio'
http://stakeholders.ofcom.org.uk/binaries/broadcast/guidance/831193/offensive-language.pdf

When Ofcom applies its statutory duty to protect the under-eighteens, it defines children as under-fifteens or aged fourteen and under. The BBC has developed its own special guidelines on making decisions about potentially offensive language in its broadcasting and online publication (http://www.bbc.co.uk/editorialguidelines/page/guidelines-harm-language/).

The field of print, online and magazine journalism in terms of its self-regulation has up until the time of writing also come to terms with setting boundaries in relation to grief, shock and suicide. The PCC issued a guidance briefing on suicide following the reporting of young people taking their own lives in Wales in 2009.

Briefing note on the reporting of suicide, March 2009
http://www.pcc.org.uk/news/index.html?article=NTU4MQ

Earlier that year the PCC upheld complaints against twelve national and local newspapers and their online news sites over their over-detailed reports of a suicide case at a coroner's inquest:

Press Complaints Commission censures 12 publications for suicide reports 05/01/2009
http://www.pcc.org.uk/news/index.html?article=NTQ2Mw
The charity, The Samaritans, has published a very helpful guide for the media on appropriate language and protocols for reporting news events involving possible suicide:
Media Guidelines for the reporting of suicide
http://www.samaritans.org/media-centre/media-guidelines-reporting-suicide'
UK Media Guidelines for reporting suicide and self-harm pdf file
http://www.samaritans.org/sites/default/files/kcfinder/files/Samaritans%20Media%20Guidelines.pdf

---

Under section 5 of the code, journalists are under a duty when covering stories involving 'personal grief or shock', to make enquiries and approaches with 'sympathy and discretion' and ensure that publications are 'handled sensitively'. Relatives should not hear of the fate of their loved ones first through media publication or journalistic enquiry.

> This requirement was established by Miss V M Oliver v *Manchester Evening News*: Report 43, 1998
> http://www.pcc.org.uk/news/index.html?article=MTg4Ng
> and Mr James McKeown v *Evening Chronicle* (Newcastle Upon Tyne)
> http://www.pcc.org.uk/news/index.html?article=MTk1OQ
> The inclusion of insensitive or unnecessary detail in a magazine's mock-up of a murder scene was censured in 2007 in the case of A man v *Chat Magazine* Report 76, 2007
> http://www.pcc.org.uk/news/index.html?article=NdgyNw
> and insensitive and unwelcome coverage of the funeral of a mother of a television personality was similarly ruled against in Smillie v *Sunday Mail*: Report 50, 2000
> http://www.pcc.org.uk/news/index.html?article=MTgyNQ

As with broadcasters the PCC has developed a self-regulatory standard on discrimination which is set out in section 12 of its Editors' Code: 'The press must avoid prejudicial or pejorative reference to an individual's race, colour, religion, gender, sexual orientation or to any physical or mental illness or disability. Details of an individual's race, colour, religion, sexual orientation, physical or mental illness or disability must be avoided unless genuinely relevant to the story.' This obligation has no qualification or exception in terms of the public interest. Issues of harm and offence are increasingly being criminally prosecuted on Twitter, Facebook, online and other social media applications. The Communications Act 2003 and Malicious Communications Act 1998 are being used against individuals and non-journalists. There were over 1,200 prosecutions in 2011 for grossly offensive and menacing communications on electronic networks. Paul Chambers had been criminally convicted after making a joke on Twitter when experiencing frustrations at an airport. The police had taken his language literally. His conviction was eventually quashed in 2012. The Director of Public Prosecutions opened a consultation into the public interest criteria for deciding how to use the criminal law in these circumstances. The political free speech debate also discussed the appropriate use of section 5 of the Public Order Act in relation to the use of threatening, abusive or insulting words or behaviour that could be seen and heard by members of the public. These laws are not yet being applied to professional journalistic publication. In December 2012 the DPP announced interim guidelines and advocated criminal prosecution only when the communication was 'more than: offensive, shocking or disturbing; or satirical, iconoclastic or rude comment; or the expression of unpopular or unfashionable opinion about serious or trivial matters, or banter or humour, even if distasteful to some or painful to those subjected to it'.

Section 127 Communications Act 2003 Improper use of public electronic communications network
http://www.legislation.gov.uk/ukpga/2003/21/section/127
Section 1 of Malicious Communications Act 1998 Letters or electronic communications with intent to cause distress or anxiety
http://www.legislation.gov.uk/ukpga/1988/27/section/1
Section 5 of the Public Order Act 1986: Harassment, alarm or distress
http://www.legislation.gov.uk/ukpga/1986/64
Chambers v Director of Public Prosecutions [2012] EWHC 2157 (Admin) (27 July 2012)
http://www.bailii.org/ew/cases/EWHC/Admin/2012/2157.html
DPP statement on Tom Daley case and social media prosecutions
http://blog.cps.gov.uk/2012/09/dpp-statement-on-tom-daley-case-and-social-media-prosecutions.html
DPP launches public consultation on prosecutions involving social media communications
http://www.cps.gov.uk/news/press_releases/dpp_launches_public_consultation_on_prosecutions_involving_social_media_communications/

★   A downloadable sound file on media law issues relating to harm and offence.
3.9 Podcast downloadable https://soundcloud.com/comparativemedialaw/podcast-3-9-the-uk-media-law

3.10 UPDATE AND STOP PRESS

These subject areas are complex, dynamic and kinetic in the sense of new case law, legislative changes and developments in media regulation. Every effort will be made to expand on and develop the various sections at the book's companion website:

http://www.ma-radio.gold.ac.uk/mediapocket/chapter3.htm

There is also an updated podcast downloadable which covers immediate news of changes and developments.

★   A downloadable sound file covering updates and developments in relation to the UK media law of libel, privacy, accuracy and balance
3.10 Podcast downloadable https://soundcloud.com/ comparativemedialaw/podcast-3-10-uk-media-law

4

NEWS GATHERING, STORY FINDING AND PUBLIC INTEREST

Bullet points summarizing news-gathering conduct that might breach the criminal law and the status of public interest defences:

- 'Public interest' definitions and doctrines used to justify breaches of primary and secondary media law
- RIPA (Regulation of Investigatory Powers Act 2000) unlawful interception of electronic radio communications, no public interest
- Computer Misuse Act 1990, no public interest
- Data Protection Act, unlawfully obtaining private information, no public interest defence
- Bribery Act, corruption, conspiring to commit misconduct in public office, theft and fraud offences, no public interest defence
- Protection of Harassment Act, defence 'for the purpose of preventing or detecting crime, complying with legal direction, and reasonable in the particular circumstances'

- PACE (Police and Criminal Evidence Act) 1984. Shields available for journalists including special court procedure required if police want media footage of public news events. Act stipulates a category of excluded material/information which is held in confidence for journalistic purposes
- Article 10 protection of sources; section 10 of 1981 Contempt of Court Act; ECtHR precedents – Goodwin, Interbrew and Dutch illegal car racers
- Venial/pardonable. Public interest exercised through discretion by CPS, DPP, courts/BBC Secret Policeman, lesser crimes committed to expose greater evils

✶ A downloadable sound file of the bullet points on potential news-gathering offences and availability of public interest defences.
4.0 Podcast downloadable https://soundcloud.com/comparativemedialaw/chapter-4-bullet-points-uk

A short video-cast on the key UK media law points concerning news gathering, story finding and public interest.
4. http://youtu.be/WZMix7z7WhE

4.1 DEFINITIONS OF THE PUBLIC INTEREST

The PCC, Ofcom, BBC, DPP and the courts all have subtly different though coinciding ideas of what constitutes 'the public interest' that would justify breaking laws in the pursuit of journalism. All future references to the PCC in this book relate to its succeeding independent regulatory body constituted following the recommendations of the 2012 Leveson Inquiry Report into the culture, practices and ethics of the press. The judgment calls will in the end be a matter for your personal conscience, the quality of decision-making by your employer and then the mercy of the investigatory and legal authorities, and even a District Judge, justices or jury at trial. The PCC sets out its understanding of the public interest at the end of its Editors' Code:

1   The public interest includes, but is not confined to:

    i   Detecting or exposing crime or serious impropriety.

    ii   Protecting public health and safety.

    iii Preventing the public from being misled by an action or statement of an individual or organisation.

2   There is a public interest in freedom of expression itself.

3   Whenever the public interest is invoked, the PCC will require editors to demonstrate fully that they reasonably believed that publication, or journalistic activity undertaken with a view to publication, would be in the public interest and how, and with whom, that was established at the time.

4   The PCC will consider the extent to which material is already in the public domain, or will become so.

5   In cases involving children under 16, editors must demonstrate an exceptional public interest to override the normally paramount interest of the child.

The PCC makes it clear that the public interest can be invoked for its sections on privacy, harassment, children, children in sex cases, hospitals, reporting crime, using clandestine devices and subterfuge, payment to criminals and those witnesses in crime cases not yet active but where it is likely and foreseeable they will be. It cannot be invoked in relation to paying witnesses likely to give evidence in active cases, breaching the confidentiality of journalists' sources, profiting by financial journalism (section 13), discriminatory publication, identifying victims of sexual assault, intrusion into grief or shock, and accuracy and giving the opportunity of reply.

Ofcom's Broadcasting Code says under section 3.5 there is 'a clear public interest' in 'investigating crime or serious wrongdoing'. Under section 8 privacy can be breached when it is 'warranted' and in the public interest and the Code says: 'Examples of public interest would include revealing or detecting crime, protecting public health or safety, exposing misleading claims made by individuals or organisations or disclosing incompetence that affects the public.'

Under section 18 of the BBC's Editorial Guidelines any breaking of the law in the process of working for the BBC is a mandatory referral duty (http://www.bbc.co.uk/editorialguidelines/page/guidelines-law-mandatory-referrals/).

The BBC does accept that there may be times when their 'accurate, impartial and fair coverage in the public interest' involves possible conflict with the law and in those circumstances it must consider: 'what effect breaking the law might have on the BBC; what the effect might be on the people concerned; internationally, the effect on the BBC's future coverage of the region'.

In the context of the 'Hackgate scandal' and Leveson Inquiry, the DPP in England and Wales has issued guidelines on how his office and the CPS would apply the public interest test when considering criminal charges against journalists. Nine non-exhaustive factors will be taken into account: (a) the impact on the victim(s) of the conduct in question, including the consequences for the victim(s); (b) whether the victim was under 18 or in a vulnerable position; (c) the overall loss and damage caused by the conduct in question; (d) whether the conduct was part of a repeated or routine pattern of behaviour or likely to continue; (e) whether there was any element of corruption in the conduct in question; (f) whether the conduct in question included the use of threats, harassment or intimidation; (g) the impact on any course of justice, for example whether a criminal investigation or proceedings may have been put in jeopardy; (h) the motivation of the suspect insofar as it can be ascertained (examples might range from malice or financial gain at one extreme to a belief that the conduct would be in the public interest at the other, taking into account the information available to the suspect at the time; (i) whether the public interest in question could equally well have been served by some lawful means having regard to all the circumstances in the particular case. After public consultation and publication of interim guidelines, the DPP finalized guidance on assessing public interest in cases affecting the media on 13 September 2012.

> Guidelines for prosecutors on assessing the public interest in cases
> affecting the media
> http://www.cps.gov.uk/legal/d_to_g/guidance_for_prosecutors_on_
> assessing_the_public_interest_in_cases_affecting_the_media_/
> Criminal offences most likely to be committed in cases affecting the
> media
> http://www.cps.gov.uk/legal/assets/uploads/files/media_guidelines_
> annex_a.pdf

✻   A downloadable sound file exploring press and broadcasting
     definitions of the public interest.
     4.1 Podcast downloadable https://soundcloud.com/
     comparativemedialaw/podcast-4-1-the-uk-media-law

4.2 POTENTIAL CRIMINAL OFFENCES AFFECTING NEWS GATHERING AND STORY FINDING

a   Section 1 of the Regulation of Investigatory Powers Act 2000
     makes it an offence to intercept another person's telecommuni-
     cations whether telephone landline, wireless or mobile phone.
     This offence is known as 'phone hacking'. When tried at a
     magistrates' court the maximum jail sentence is six months,
     but if tried at the Crown Court the imprisonment can be as
     much as two years. There is no public interest defence for
     journalists.
b   Section 1 of the Computer Misuse Act 1990 makes it an
     offence to gain access to another person's computer without
     their permission whether by use of Trojan virus, using a pass-
     word or simply logging on. Guessing the password of another
     person's email account and accessing their email would be a
     criminal offence under the Act. This is known as 'computer
     hacking' and is triable either way with a maximum of six
     months' imprisonment on conviction at the magistrates' court
     and two years on indictment at the Crown Court. There is no
     public interest defence available for journalists.
c   Section 55 of the Data Protection Act 1998 makes it an offence

to unlawfully gain access to private information. When journalists obtain the information by subterfuge the trick is known as 'blagging'. There is a defence available for journalists acting in the public interest. The crime can only be prosecuted at the magistrates' court with a maximum fine of £5,000. The Leveson Inquiry Report recommended reform of the Act to change the public interest defence for journalists so that a breach would need to be necessary for publication, rather than simply being in fact undertaken with a view to publication. The report advocated introducing compensation for pure distress to victims as well as pecuniary loss and custodial penalties in addition to existing fines for journalists found guilty of committing offences.

d   Up until 2010 bribing a police officer or public employee was a criminal offence under the Prevention of Corruption Act 1906. The Metropolitan Police enquiries into 'Hackgate' have pursued 1906 Corruption Act offences in respect of alleged payments to non-police officers and in theory could include any civil servant. After the enactment of the 2010 Bribery Act, such offences are dealt with by the new legislation. The maximum sentence is now ten years' imprisonment and/or an unlimited fine. The conduct element is when a journalist may offer, promise or give a financial or other advantage to another person. The statute is drafted with a wide ambit.

The Bribery Act 2010 Guidance from the Ministry of Justice
http://www.justice.gov.uk/downloads/legislation/bribery-act–2010-guidance.pdf

---

e   Misconduct in public office is a common law offence and journalists can be accused of conspiring to incite, abet or aid a public official, civil servant or police officer to commit misconduct in public office. The official has to act without justification or legal excuse, and the wilful misconduct must amount to an abuse of the public trust. In theory the maximum sentence is life, but sentencing practice requires judges to apply penalties that are proportionate to the circumstances and previous case law. Statutory conspiracy under section 1 of the 1977 Criminal Law Act is triable on indictment only at the Crown Court and carries the maximum penalty for the substantive offence. There is no public interest defence available for journalists committing corruption or bribery offences, or conspiring to incite misconduct in public office. This is also true for knowingly destroying evidence in a cover-up to subvert or frustrate a police inquiry to avoid arrest which could amount to the common law offence of perverting the course of justice, again carrying a maximum of life imprisonment and unlimited fine. There is no journalistic public interest defence.

f   The Protection of Harassment Act 1997 makes it a criminal offence for a journalist to repeatedly doorstep an individual in such a way as to cause distress on at least two occasions. This protects people in the news and public figures from 'media scrums' or being 'besieged'. There is a defence in the legislation if it can be shown that the reporter's actions were 'for the purpose of preventing or detecting crime, complying with legal direction, and reasonable in the particular circumstances'. A civil case in 2001 at the Court of Appeal involving a civilian worker for the City of London police called Esther Thomas demonstrated that media publication could amount to harassment under the legislation. In that case *The Sun* newspaper had invited readers to express their views about Ms Thomas's decision to report racist behaviour by City of London police officers. The enactment of a new criminal offence of stalking in the Protection of Freedoms Act 2012 widens the range of harassing conduct that can be defined as criminal. In theory the legislation could be used against the media as there is no public interest defence for the purposes of news gathering.

Section 111 of the Protection of Freedoms Act: Offences in relation to stalking
http://www.legislation.gov.uk/ukpga/2012/9/section/111/enacted
Thomas v News Group Newspapers Ltd & Anor [2001] EWCA Civ 1233 (18 July 2001)
http://www.bailii.org/ew/cases/EWCA/Civ/2001/1233.html

g   Under the Serious Crime Act 2007, sections 44 to 46, it is possible that journalists researching and reporting with people committing crimes could find themselves at risk of prosecution for 'intentionally encouraging or assisting an offence', and doing the same 'believing it will be committed'. The penalties on conviction could be equivalent to those imposed for the crime that was assisted and encouraged.

h   Other crimes and understanding the pardonable and venial. There is a common law concept of criminal misconduct by journalists when investigating more serious crimes being considered 'venial' or pardonable by the courts. This is taking into account the public interest in permitting criminal wrongdoing if it checks or exposes a greater evil. The process requires an exercise of discretion by the police, CPS, DPP or the courts (see Section 4.1) An example in recent years of a decision not to proceed with a criminal prosecution against a journalist is the case of the BBC's 2003 undercover documentary 'The Secret Policeman' when investigative reporter Mark Daly joined the Greater Manchester Police as a probationer constable and surreptitiously filmed instances of racist attitude on the part of fellow police cadets. He was initially arrested for obtaining pecuniary advantage by deception, which would now be a 'fraud offence' and criminally damaging a police uniform, but the case was not proceeded with. In undercover work, any journalist applying for and getting a job using a false identity and fake qualifications should be under the supervision of a qualified and expert media lawyer and it is advisable that the salary and any other financial benefits are paid into a separate bank account to be returned to the employer at the end of the journalistic investigation. News organizations should exercise great care when receiving mobiles or computers handed in by members of the public. Any evidence indicating that journalists suspected or had good reason for believing the items had been stolen could generate a liability for theft offences, particularly if steps were taken to examine and gain access to the data on the electronic devices. Every action moves the liability into other fields of potential criminal wrongdoing. The police would be looking for any evidence of intention to permanently deprive the rightful owner of the items and their statutory rights in respect of the information on the devices.

★   A downloadable sound file describing criminal offences that could be committed while news gathering or carrying out journalistic research.
4.2 Podcast downloadable https://soundcloud.com/comparativemedialaw/podcast-4-2-the-uk-media-law

4.3 PROTECTING SOURCES

Section 10 of the 1981 Contempt of Court Act states:

> No court may require a person to disclose, nor is any person guilty of contempt of court for refusing to disclose, the source of information contained in a publication for which he is responsible unless it is established to the satisfaction of the court that it is necessary in the interests of justice or national security or for the prevention of disorder or crime.

This is a statutory legal protection for journalists despite the qualifications. The PCC Editors' Code declares under section 14: 'Journalists have a moral obligation to protect confidential sources of information.' The National Union of Journalists under section 7 of its code of ethics asserts that a member must protect 'the identity of sources who supply information in confidence and material gathered in the course of her/his work'. The Chartered Institute of Journalists' code of conduct stipulates under rule 7 that its members 'will maintain the confidences you agreed with any contributors'. Under rule 9 members are expected 'to check sources and understand that previously published material may not always have been created using the exacting standards of a professional journalist and will independently seek to verify that the information is accurate'. Members are also bound under rule 10 'to defend the principles of a free press and freedom of speech and will do nothing to damage these principles'.

The death of Dr David Kelly in 2003 after being the BBC's source for an allegation that a government dossier had exaggerated the military threat to the United Kingdom from Iraq's weapons of mass destruction led to a high-profile inquiry under Lord Hutton. The criticism of the BBC's handling of the story and its source led to the resignations of the reporter Andrew Gilligan, Director General Greg Dyke and also the chair of the then BBC Board of Governors. The subsequent internal BBC inquiry report compiled by a committee headed by Ronald Neil sets out the BBC's recognition of professional duties and standards in its handling of sources.

> The editorial lessons for the BBC arising out of the Hutton Enquiry
> http://downloads.bbc.co.uk/aboutthebbc/insidethebbc/howwework/
> reports/pdf/neil_report.pdf

Journalists are entitled to some protection against police powers of search and seizure. Under the Police and Criminal Evidence Act 1984, 'excluded material' includes 'journalistic material acquired or created for the purposes of journalism'. Excluded material is information and writing (notebooks or computerized information) that is held in confidence. Journalistic excluded material is defined by Part II, section 11 of the Act:

> http://www.legislation.gov.uk/ukpga/1984/60/section/11

The Leveson Inquiry Report urged the Home Office to consider repealing the protection of sources provision in Schedule 1 of the Police and Criminal Evidence Act 1984 and amend it in order to define the phrase 'for the purposes of journalism'. The report argued that the protection of confidential journalistic material should only apply if possessed continuously 'since it was first acquired or created subject to an enforceable or lawful undertaking, restriction or obligation'. This phraseology, if enacted, could reduce the shield for information given to a journalist by anyone breaking the law. The Report also advocated a data trail for any contact between police officers and journalists with ACPO members being obliged to record 'all of their contact with the media, and for that record to be available publicly for transparency and audit purposes'.

Journalistic material not held in confidence is also protected in that the police have to use a special procedure to obtain a 'production order'. This is set out in Part II section 14 of the Act:

> http://www.legislation.gov.uk/ukpga/1984/60/section/14

Only a circuit judge can give the police permission to seize such material through a court application. However, this protection is not absolute. The police can override these shields when investigating serious criminal offences such as terrorism and espionage and there are legal powers for courts to grant search and seizure warrants without the media being given notice or the opportunity to challenge the application. A useful watershed precedent, where the courts supported journalists over the police investigating alleged breaches of the Official Secrets Act, involved the then *Observer* reporter Martin Bright and former MI5 officer David Shayler:

> *Bright, R (on the application of) v Central Criminal Court* [2000] EWHC 560 (QB) (21 July 2000)
> http://www.bailii.org/cgi-bin/markup.cgi?doc=/ew/cases/EWHC/QB/2000/560.html

Most photographic and film material acquired through reporting requires special procedure if the police wish to seize it. Media organizations are acutely concerned that regular police seizure of its footage and the courts' agreement to give access to it will expose front-line media workers to violence, attack and intimidation at public order and conflict events. A ruling against the police over material gathered in the eviction of residents from the Dale Farm travellers' site in October 2011 has been hailed as an important precedent requiring judges to 'give sufficient weight to the inhibiting effect of production orders on the press'.

> *British Sky Broadcasting Ltd & Ors, R (on the application of) v Chelmsford Crown Court* [2012] EWHC 1295 (Admin) (17 May 2012)
> http://www.bailii.org/cgi-bin/markup.cgi?doc=/ew/cases/EWHC/Admin/2012/1295.html

My practical advice in relation to special procedure and excluded material is to label any news-gathering devices you use when reporting in the field 'Special material under PACE 1984' and if any attempt is made by the police to 'seize' it, to politely point out your role as a legitimate journalist and their need to make an application to a judge. Any physical resistance is not recommended under any circumstances. In these situations you need a professional media lawyer and representation. Similarly, should you face police arrest and the search of your home and work premises you should signpost the status of any records you have that are confidential to your work as a journalist and could undermine the protection you have for your sources. Again you should avoid obstructing the police or physically resisting them. But you are entitled to protest and assert your professional and constitutional status. You are entitled to the evaluation of an independent court examination of the merits of the police action.

The European Court of Human Rights (ECtHR) has asserted the importance of protecting journalists' sources under Article 10 freedom of expression in the 1996 case of journalist William Goodwin, who was fined for refusing to disclose the source of a story about a computer software company's finances.

> *Goodwin v The United Kingdom* App no. 17488/90 [1996] ECtHR 16 (27 March 1996) Grand Chamber ruling
> http://www.bailii.org/eu/cases/ECHR/1996/16.html

The ECtHR affirmed this principle in the legal dispute between the *Financial Times* and others with the Belgian company Interbrew in a 2009 ruling.

> *Financial Times Ltd and Others v The United Kingdom* App no. 821/03
> [2009] ECtHR 2065 (15 December 2009)
> http://www.bailii.org/eu/cases/ECHR/2009/2065.html

Another significant ruling of the ECtHR Grand Chamber in 2010 in favour of the Dutch magazine *Autoweek*, which had been ordered to hand over photographs of an illegal car racing event to the police, continued the strong protection of journalist sources.

> *Sanoma Uitgevers B.V. v The Netherlands* App no. 38224/03 [2010]
> ECtHR 1284 (14 September 2010)
> http://www.bailii.org/eu/cases/ECHR/2010/1284.html

The Terrorism Act 2000 and Anti-Terrorism, Crime and Security Act 2001 have created new offences of 'withholding information on suspected terrorist offences'. A journalist faces prosecution if during the course of his/her work he/she fails to report the discovery of information about terrorism or 'he/she knows or believes he/she might be of material assistance in preventing the commission by another person of an act of terrorism, or in securing the apprehension, prosecution or conviction of another person in the UK for an offence involving the commission, preparation or instigation of an act of terrorism'.

The ability of journalists to protect their sources is under intense threat in the context of the power structures in British society at the time of writing. I set out the implications of the death of Dr David Kelly in a *British Journalism Review* article in 2003, which is available online:

> 'Is your source ever really safe?' *British Journalism Review* Vol. 14, No.
> 4, 2003, pages 7–12
> http://www.bjr.org.uk/data/2003/no4_crook

I think it would be wise to provide caveats to guarantees to confidential sources and demonstrate good professional practice and a sincere intention to use best endeavours etc. Obviously counter-surveillance measures such as avoiding email/digital communications, digital trails to meetings, the use of pay-as-you-go mobiles as well as proxy services and encryption of digital messaging and storage would be helpful. The private security industry serves powerful corporations, oligarchs, celebrocrats, and organized crime syndicates that can buy the best surveillance and information-gathering resources, whether legal or unlawful. In addition the British state and all its government bodies have information-gathering powers that can reach everywhere. The intelligence structure has informants (most unpaid) and access to anything held or processed in key and significant UK news and journalism publishers. In 2012–13 the UK Parliament was considering provisions in the Communications and Data Bill that proposed retention of all Internet and email material to be accessible to the law enforcement agencies. A critical parliamentary committee report highlighted the risks caused by this extension of state surveillance and indeed the difficulties journalists face in the digital age of maintaining the confidence of their sources and information.

Report of the Joint Committee on the Draft Communications Data Bill December 11 2012
http://www.parliament.uk/business/committees/committees-a-z/
joint-select/draft-communications-bill/news/full-publication-of-report/
Cleland Thom 'Why investigative journalists may need to use a pseudonym on 192.com'
http://www.pressgazette.co.uk/content/
why-investigative-journalists-may-need-use-pseudonym-192com

✻   A downloadable sound file on key statutory and case law protection of sources.
4.3 Podcast downloadable https://soundcloud.com/
comparativemedialaw/podcast-4-3-the-uk-media-law

4.4 SECONDARY MEDIA LAW AND REGULATION

The Press Complaints Commission, BBC Editorial Guidelines, and Ofcom Broadcasting Code indicate that the media can be justified in invading the privacy of individuals and organizations by using subterfuge and secret/surreptitious recording when they are acting in the public interest and investigating crime. This is recognized by all three codes. Another stipulation is that the journalist cannot obtain the evidence and information by any other method of research and reporting. If aggressive and persistent doorstepping in order to obtain a comment or interview from anyone who has made it clear they have nothing to say is judged by the police not to be unlawful, secondary media law is more likely to be applied. Section 4 of the Editors' Code entitled 'Harassment' stipulates that journalists 'must not engage in intimidation, harassment or persistent pursuit', and must not persist 'in questioning, telephoning, pursuing or photographing individuals once asked to desist; nor remain on their property when asked to leave'. They must not follow people who have been asked to be left alone and if requested 'must identify themselves and whom they represent'. Editors are urged to ensure these standards are upheld by their reporters and staff and 'non-compliant' material acquired from agencies and freelances should not be used for publication. The BBC Editorial Guidelines on 'doorstepping' provide a comprehensive briefing on the duties of broadcasters to comply with best practice standards in this area (http://www.bbc.co.uk/editorialguidelines/page/guidelines-privacy-doorstepping/). This is also true of the technique of secret recording (http://www.bbc.co.uk/editorialguidelines/page/guidelines-privacy-practices-secret-recording/). The PCC Editors' Code warns that there has to be public interest justification under section 10 for 'using hidden cameras or clandestine listening devices; or by intercepting private or mobile telephone calls, messages or emails; or by the unauthorised removal of documents or photographs; or by accessing digitally-held private information without consent'. Like Ofcom, the PCC stipulates that engaging in misrepresentation or subterfuge whether by journalists or 'by agents or intermediaries' can generally be justified only in the public interest and 'when the material cannot be obtained by other means'. The phone hacking scandal and multiple police enquiries arising out of it have demonstrated that where media regulation fails, public anger and criminal investigation follow.

✴   A downloadable sound file on secondary media law obligations in relation to information and news-gathering practices in journalism.
4.4 Podcast downloadable https://soundcloud.com/comparativemedialaw/podcast-4-4-the-uk-media-law

4.5   UPDATES AND STOP PRESS

More information and updates also on the companion website http://www.ma-radio.gold.ac.uk/mediapocketbook/chapter4

✴   A downloadable sound file updating the reader on developments in the media law of news gathering and definitions of public interest.
4.5 Pocast downloadable https://soundcloud.com/comparativemedialaw/podcast-4-5-the-uk-media-law

5

PROTECTING CHILDREN

Key legal points and concepts protecting children from media harm, intrusion and identification:

- Children and young people are a special case in primary and secondary media law enjoying considerable statutory and case law protection in terms of anonymity in the criminal justice system
- Children and young people have special protection in the Ofcom Broadcasting Code
- Children and young people are given very high priority in privacy case law in the balancing act between Article 10 and Article 8 ECHR
- Independent press regulation draws from an Editors' Code that gives children and young people very high-priority protection
- Photographers, online image editors, and visual broadcasters have to realize that the depiction of children and young people requires understanding of prohibitions, consent and anonymizing

> • The considerable restrictions in family law and family court proceedings are designed to protect the welfare and interests of children

✱ A downloadable sound file of bullet points summarizing media law protection for children.
5.0 Podcast downloadable https://soundcloud.com/comparativemedialaw/chapter-5-bulletpoints-the-uk

---

A short video-cast explaining key UK media law points on the protection of children
5. video-cast http://youtu.be/CbYig2gEopk

5.1   CHILDREN IN THE CRIMINAL JUSTICE SYSTEM

The age of criminal responsibility in England and Wales is ten – one of the lowest in Europe. In the English adult courts youths aged 17 and under can have anonymity if an order is made under the Children and Young Persons Act 1933 – known as 'Section 39 Orders'. This applies to witnesses and defendants. It is inconceivable that any living child sex offence victim could be identified. Child sex offence complainants, like adults, have statutory anonymity for life from the time an allegation has been made. Furthermore child sexual offence complainants under the age of 16 cannot waive their right to anonymity. It can only be lifted by order of a court.

It might be argued that Section 39 anonymity orders in the adult courts do not serve much purpose if the alleged victim is a baby or so young as not to be conscious of the effect of publicity i.e. under around four years of age, but the courts will still be conscious of the victim's future welfare and dignity. The orders should not be made if the child victim is deceased. Courts are supposed to balance the interests of open justice and the welfare of the children affected.

> *Y, R (on the application of) v Aylesbury Crown Court & Ors* [2012] EWHC
> 1140 (Admin) (01 May 2012)
> http://www.bailii.org/ew/cases/EWHC/Admin/2012/1140.html

As indicated in a previous chapter it is important to watch out for jigsaw identification – e.g. when one media organization reports the case of a parent neglecting his or her child and a Section 39 Order has been made on the victim. Obviously if one media outlet reports that parents neglected their children and another reports identified adults for being cruel to children in their care, the audience is likely to appreciate the connection. One policy is needed by all media for the reporting of the case and furthermore the nature of the agreed detail in the reporting must avoid the publication of anything construed in law as 'particulars calculated to lead' to the identification of the child protected by the order.

> *Gazette Media Company Ltd & Ors, R (on the application of) v Teesside
> Crown Court* [2005] EWCA Crim 1983 (26 July 2005)
> http://www.bailii.org/cgi-bin/markup.cgi?doc=/ew/cases/EWCA/
> Crim/2005/1983.html

Most crimes committed by people aged 17 and under are dealt with in a separate system of 'Youth Courts', or by local authority protection orders. There is normally default anonymity for youths in the Youth Courts under section 49 of the Children and Young Persons Act 1933 and a prohibition on identifying anything that could lead to the identification of the youths or the schools they go to. Only reporters are permitted access to Youth Court proceedings. Section 45 of the Crime (Sentences) Act 1997 gave Youth Courts the power to remove anonymity in the public interest:

> Lifting restrictions on reports of proceedings in which children or
> young persons are concerned
> http://www.legislation.gov.uk/ukpga/1997/43/section/45

If a youth reaches the age of 18 during proceedings the statutory anonymity under the Children and Young Persons Act 1933 can no longer apply.

Anti-Social Behaviour Orders (known as ASBOs) are applied for by local authorities with the support of the police. These are technically civil proceedings. There was a political dimension to the legislation in that courts should have the power to identify youths receiving these orders in order that the community could be alerted to troublesome youths who should not be at large in shopping centres or banned areas. ASBOs are usually made by adult magistrates' courts and they would have to issue a Section 39 Order if they wish the youths to enjoy anonymity. If youths breach ASBOs they are dealt with by Youth Courts in criminal proceedings, and section 141 of the Serious Organised Crime and Police Act 2005 meant that youths in these cases could be identified unless the court wished to impose anonymity.

ASBOs: reporting restrictions when appearing in Youth Courts for committing the criminal offence of breaching the order
http://www.legislation.gov.uk/ukpga/2005/15/section/141

The situation has been complicated by the fact that Parliament has also given Youth Courts the power to impose ASBOs on young offenders at the same time they are convicted of criminal offences. In this situation journalists would have to apply to the court for Section 49 default restrictions to be lifted if they wished to identify the youths concerned.

In 2012 the UK government was intending to replace ASBOs with Criminal Behaviour Orders and Crime Prevention Injunctions. It is unclear if the reporting restriction rules would remain the same for the new regime.

Home Office consultation on criminal behaviour orders
http://www.homeoffice.gov.uk/publications/consultations/
asb-consultation/criminal-behaviour-order

★ A downloadable sound file explaining the restrictions available for children in the English (and Welsh) criminal justice system.
5.1 Podcast downloadable https://soundcloud.com/comparativemedialaw/podcast-5-1-the-uk-media-law

5.2 OFCOM AND UK BROADCASTING 'PROTECTING THE UNDER-EIGHTEENS'

The first section of Ofcom's Broadcasting Code is dedicated to protecting people under the age of 18 whether they are regarded as children, young people or youths. A flavour of the mission is clear in section 1.1: 'Material that might seriously impair the physical, mental or moral development of people under eighteen must not be broadcast.'

Section 1: Protecting the Under-Eighteens
http://stakeholders.ofcom.org.uk/broadcasting/broadcast-codes/broadcast-code–2008/protectingu18/

Essentially UK broadcasting operates a watershed for television set at 21.00 and consequently language and content is measured and adjudicated on its harm and offence potential in relation to viewers aged 17 and under. Similar protection is applied to radio listeners though the risk period of transmission is determined when 'children are particularly likely to be listening'.

Ofcom enforces any harm caused by jigsaw identification and is likely to investigate breaches of reporting restrictions.

The Code deals with reporting of children and crime outside the ambit of primary media law in section 1.9:

> When covering any pre-trial investigation into an alleged criminal offence in the UK, broadcasters should pay particular regard to the potentially vulnerable position of any person who is not yet adult who is involved as a witness or victim, before broadcasting their name, address, identity of school or other educational establishment, place

of work, or any still or moving picture of them. Particular justification is also required for the broadcast of such material relating to the identity of any person who is not yet adult who is involved in the defence as a defendant or potential defendant.

The BBC Editorial Guidelines are equally stringent in protecting young people through its broadcasting and online publishing and it is worth noting that Ofcom does not regulate the online content activities of its licensees. The BBC articulates an additional duty to children and young people as contributors:

BBC Editorial Guidelines Section 9: Children and Young People as Contributors
http://www.bbc.co.uk/editorialguidelines/page/guidelines-children-introduction/
Full attention needs to be paid to the BBC's policy on mandatory referrals in this area:
http://www.bbc.co.uk/editorialguidelines/page/guidelines-children-mandatory-referrals/

✳ A downloadable sound file voicing this section on the Ofcom and BBC policy of protecting young people aged under eighteen. 5.2 Podcast downloadable https://soundcloud.com/comparativemedialaw/podcast-5-2-the-uk-media-law

5.3 HIGH PRIORITY FOR CARE OF CHILDREN IN PRIVACY CASE LAW

It has to be recognized how judicial supervision and legal care of children ripples out and leads to restrictions on the identification and open justice revelations concerning adults in criminal trials and wider frames of social communication. In the balancing exercise to what extent are children the trump card against freedom of expression? This is an interesting debating topic and the answer is unresolved. There are two case histories demonstrating the methodology of the UK courts and how balancing these human rights is resolved on its merits rather than attention to absolute principles.

S (a child), Re [2004] UKHL 47 (28 October 2004)
http://www.bailii.org/uk/cases/UKHL/2004/47.html
A Local Authority v W [2005] EWHC 1564 (Fam) (14 July 2005)
http://www.bailii.org/ew/cases/EWHC/Fam/2005/1564.html

✷   A downloadable sound file setting out the high priority given
    to the care of children in privacy cases heard in the UK
    courts.
    5.3 Podcast downloadable https://soundcloud.com/
    comparativemedialaw/podcast-5-3-the-uk-media-law

5.4 INDEPENDENT PRESS REGULATION – HIGH PROTECTION OF CHILDREN

Independent press regulation Section 6 of the Editors' Code
commits print and online journalists to recognizing that 'young
people should be free to complete their time at school without
unnecessary intrusion'. A child under 16 must not be interviewed
or photographed on issues involving their own or another child's
welfare unless a custodial parent or similarly responsible adult
consents. Pupils must not be approached or photographed at school
without the permission of the school authorities. Minors must not
be paid for material involving children's welfare, nor parents or
guardians for material about their children or wards, unless it is
clearly in the child's interest. Editors must not use the fame, noto-
riety or position of a parent or guardian as sole justification for
publishing details of a child's private life. The Editors' Codebook by
Ian Beales warns that children should be treated with care and
this applies to anyone up to the age of 16, and higher in relation
to school education. In a decision in 2002 it was not enough that a
child's mother had consented to her son's picture being taken while
at school. Permission from the school was needed.

Mr Colin Eves, the headmaster of Brecon High School v Brecon and
Radnor Express: Report 57, 2002
http://www.pcc.org.uk/news/index.html?article=MjA2Ng

✳   A downloadable sound file on the high protection of children
       afforded by independent press regulation in the UK.
       5.4 Podcast downloadable https://soundcloud.com/
       comparativemedialaw/podcast-5-4-the-uk-media-law

5.5   CHILDREN AND PICTURES

Still and moving pictures of children in the UK media require the
informed consent of parents and supervising adults *in loco parentis*.
Any image that could be construed or interpreted as an indecent
image of a person aged 17 and under is likely to be a serious criminal offence in the UK. Anyone taking or in possession of such an
image in any form, transmitting, editing or publishing it, is liable to
prosecution. The *Editors' Codebook* states categorically that children
under the age of 16 'cannot be photographed on issues involving
their own or another child's welfare without a custodial parent's or
guardian's consent, or at school without the school's permission'.
The balancing exercise adopted by broadcasters to comply with
the Broadcasting Code in relation to pictorial representation of
young people, even when concealment editing has been applied
and permission to use the footage not obtained, can be complicated. The decision of Ofcom's Fairness Committee in 2005 in a
case involving undercover filming in a school is illustrative of the
approach and analysis involved:

> Broadcast Bulletin Issue number 77 – 29 January 2007, Complaint
> by Ms V on behalf of her daughter (a Minor) 'Dispatches', *Channel 4*,
> 7 July 2005
> http://stakeholders.ofcom.org.uk/enforcement/broadcast-bulletins/
> obb77/

✳   A downloadable sound file briefly exploring key primary and
       secondary media law relating to children and media images.
       5.5 Podcast downloadable https://soundcloud.com/
       comparativemedialaw/podcast-5-5-the-uk-media-law

5.6 CHILDREN AND FAMILY COURTS

Children who are wards of court and in local authority care cannot be identified as the subject of matrimonial/Children Act proceedings, or any other custody disputes. It may be possible to give publicity to a child who is a ward of court where the event or issue bears no relation to the proceedings. This is a very complicated area of media law and although the Judicial College and the Society of Editors have published a comprehensive briefing on 'Reporting the Family Courts', I would advise obtaining specialist advice before publishing stories from this field. The key legislative restrictions derive from section 12 of the 1960 Administration of Justice Act and section 97 of the 1989 Children Act and other related statutes such as the 2002 Adoption and Children Act.

Section 12 Administration of Justice Act 1960 Publication of information relating to proceedings in private:
http://www.legislation.gov.uk/ukpga/Eliz2/8-9/65
Section 97 Children Act 1989 Privacy for children involved in certain proceedings:
http://www.legislation.gov.uk/ukpga/1989/41/section/97
Section 1 Judicial Proceedings (Restriction on Reports) Act 1926 Restriction on publication of reports of judicial proceeding:
http://www.legislation.gov.uk/ukpga/Geo5/16-17/61/section/1

Should you be admitted to a family hearing as a journalist or be given information about a 'private hearing' you did not attend, you must obtain clarification about the restrictions that apply to the reporting. There may be more things you can report than you realize. For example section 12(2) of the 1960 Administration of Justice Act provides that the publication of the text or a summary of the whole or part of an order made by a court sitting in private shall not be a contempt of court unless prohibited by the court. Usually the judgment of courts in family proceedings in the High Court or the Court of Protection released for public dissemination have restricted matters redacted. If you are reporting a family/divorce or matrimonial proceeding you are usually severely restricted to reporting the following four categories of information: the names, addresses and occupations of the parties and witnesses; a concise statement of the charges, defences and countercharges in support of which evidence has been given (or equivalent); submissions on any point of law arising in the course of the proceedings and the decision of the court thereon; the summing-up of the judge and the findings of the jury (if any and highly unlikely) and the judgment of the court and observations made by the judge in giving judgment. What this means is that reporting the detail of the evidence is a likely contempt of court. But clearly the detail of the judge's ruling will be reportable subject to any additional restrictions.

Examples of family court rulings released to the media
Norfolk County Council v Webster & Ors [2006] EWHC 2733 (Fam) (01 November 2006)
http://www.bailii.org/ew/cases/EWHC/Fam/2006/2733.html
Re E (Medical treatment: Anorexia) (Rev 1) [2012] EWHC 1639 (COP) (15 June 2012)
http://www.bailii.org/ew/cases/EWHC/COP/2012/1639.html
The Family Courts: Media Access & Reporting July 2011
http://www.judiciary.gov.uk/Resources/JCO/Documents/Guidance/family-courts-media-july2011.pdf

---

✶   A downloadable sound file summarizing in brief terms the restrictions applying to family proceedings and the protection of the children involved in the cases.
5.6 Podcast downloadable https://soundcloud.com/comparativemedialaw/podcast-5-6-the-uk-media-law

5.7   UPDATES AND STOP PRESS

Every effort will be made to expand on and develop the various sections at the book's companion website:

---

http://www.ma-radio.gold.ac.uk/mediapocketbook/chapter5.

There is also an updated downloadable podcast which covers immediate news of changes and developments:

✱   A downloadable sound file maintaining an update on developments in primary and secondary media law concerning the protection of children.
5.7 Podcast downloadable https://soundcloud.com/comparativemedialaw/podcast-5-7-the-uk-media-law

6

COPYRIGHT AND INTELLECTUAL PROPERTY

Five key bullet points summarizing UK copyright for media publishers:

- Copyright and intellectual property (IP) is a complex area of media law affecting every aspect of a media communicator's work in terms of sourcing material for publication.
- Most journalists and media communicators depend on the fair dealing defence of using material for the purpose of reporting current events or criticism and review
- There is no fair dealing defence for the use of images when reporting current events and it is very limited in relation to criticism and review
- UK IP law is not as flexible as that of the USA, is increasingly influenced from the European Union and usually lasts 70 years from the death of the author
- Online and Internet technology make copyright infringement easier as well as the infringement easier to detect and legally challenge

★   A downloadable sound file vocalizing bullet points on British
     intellectual property law.
     6.0 Podcast downloadable https://soundcloud.com/
     comparativemedialaw/chapter-6-bullet-points-the-uk

> A short video-cast explaining key UK media law points on copyright
> and intellectual property
> 6. video-cast http://youtu.be/gbP-52lw1Gs

6.1 EXPLAINING UK COPYRIGHT AND FAIR DEALING

Copyright is divided between: (a) authorial/primary works (LDMA
standing for: Literary, Dramatic, Musical and Artistic), and (b)
entrepreneurial/derivative/secondary works (SFBCT standing
for: Sound recordings, Films, Broadcasts, Cable programmes,
Typographical works).

There is copyright in iconic designs that are the logos of public
and private corporations. For example the design of the London
Underground map is copyrighted.

There is copyright in tables, lists/compilations, computer
programs and databases. This is where the process of compila-
tion can be seen as requiring skill, creativity and/or labour. This is
why listings of television/radio programmes are copyrighted and
licensed. Other examples include a bus timetable, or a directory of
the top 20 classical tunes. The controlling legislation for copyright
is the 1988 Copyright Designs and Patents Act with subsequent
amendments – mainly from EU directives and regulations.

> http://www.legislation.gov.uk/ukpga/1988/48/contents

The idea/expression dichotomy is a concept dealing with the
fact that there is no copyright in facts and ideas; however if somebody has written an expression of researched facts and imaginative ideas then your substantial use of that is likely to be a breach

of their copyright. One of the most dramatic case histories on this issue involved the novel *The Da Vinci Code* by Dan Brown.

Baigent & Anor v The Random House Group Ltd [2007] EWCA Civ 247 (28 March 2007)
http://www.bailii.org/cgi-bin/markup.cgi?doc=/ew/cases/EWCA/ Civ/2007/247.html

Bear in mind that rewriting somebody else's work and representing it as your own could also undermine the original author's moral rights.

'Moral rights' are enacted in Chapter 4 of the 1988 Copyright, Designs and Patents Act and enable an author to assert the right to be identified as the author of a text. If as a publisher you have the copyright owner's permission to reproduce the work, the legal duty to identify the actual authorship remains. The legislation gives authors the right to object to any derogatory treatment of their work and this can include deletion, addition and alteration impacting on the author's reputation. Any published derogatory treatment of an author's work can amount to an infringement of 'moral rights'. It is important to understand that 'moral rights' unlike copyright itself, cannot be assigned or licensed. They always remain with the author.

Copyright, Designs and Patents Act 1988, Chapter IV Moral Rights
Right to be identified as author or director
http://www.legislation.gov.uk/ukpga/1988/48/part/I/chapter/IV

If there has been a public interest news/current event covered by television channel(s) you might think it is possible to take a screen-grab of the footage while it is current for the purposes of reporting. However, you will need to get permission and it will require attribution as to the source. There is case law allowing short video clips to be used for news/current events/criticism/ review reporting/programme where the source has been attributed and it has been shown that the use does not undermine the commercial exploitation potential invested in by the original copyright owner. In other words you are not undermining the right of the copyright owner to derive an income from the material. This is known as fair dealing. The current reporting has to be within 24 hours of the event. However, screen-grabs of YouTube videos that are merely illustrative of a story you might be writing are in copyright. Permission is needed from authors/producers. The UK Copyright Service provides a wide range of explanatory resources for copyright and intellectual property law.

http://www.copyrightservice.co.uk/copyright/uk_law_summary

Since this area of media law engages a high commodification and profit value in information, entertainments and communications products, the industry is very active in pursuing infringement and in particular websites that provide links to pirated in-copyright materials. From October 2012, the London Patents Court initiated a small claims court process for copyright owners who wished to pursue infringement remedies up to the value of £5,000. This facility is likely to be extended elsewhere and will enable freelance photographers and small media businesses to follow a low-cost route to secure legal compensation for breaching of their IP rights. The Federation Against Copyright Theft known as 'FACT' is an organization that undertakes private prosecutions where the CPS is unsuccessful.

http://www.fact-uk.org.uk/

✶   A downloadable sound file summarizing the principles of UK copyright and 'fair dealing'.
6.1 Podcast downloadable https://soundcloud.com/comparativemedialaw/podcast-6-1-the-uk-media-law

6.2 FAIR DEALING DEFENCE IN DETAIL AND UNDERSTANDING ITS EXCLUSION FROM PHOTOGRAPHS

You need to understand the UK fair dealing defence under section 30 of the Copyright, Designs and Patents Act 1988 as subsequently amended:

---

http://www.legislation.gov.uk/ukpga/1988/48/section/30

---

30 Criticism, review and news reporting

1   Fair dealing with a work for the purpose of criticism or review, of that or another work or of a performance of a work, does not infringe any copyright in the work provided that it is accompanied by a sufficient acknowledgement [F1 and provided that the work has been made available to the public].

[F2(1A) For the purposes of subsection (1) a work has been made available to the public if it has been made available by any means, including—

a   the issue of copies to the public;

b   making the work available by means of an electronic retrieval system;

c   the rental or lending of copies of the work to the public;

d   the performance, exhibition, playing or showing of the work in public;

e   the communication to the public of the work;

but in determining generally for the purposes of that subsection whether a work has been made available to the public no account shall be taken of any unauthorised act.]

2   Fair dealing with a work (other than a photograph) for the purpose of reporting current events does not infringe any copyright in the work provided that (subject to subsection (3)) it is accompanied by a sufficient acknowledgement.

3   No acknowledgement is required in connection with the reporting of current events by means of a sound recording, film [F3 or broadcast where this would be impossible for reasons of practicality or otherwise].

In relation to photographs there is no fair dealing defence for the purpose of reporting current events, but there is a very limited and circumscribed fair dealing defence for the purpose of criticism or review (section 30(1)). The photograph or photographs have to be subject to criticism or review and that purpose in the publication must be clear. The photograph/photographs must have been available to the public as set out in section 30(1)(a)–(e). The authors/owners of the copyright must be acknowledged/attributed, and the criticism/review publication must not prejudice the copyright owner's commercial interests.

Fraser-Woodward Ltd v British Broadcasting Corporation Brighter Pictures Ltd [2005] EWHC 472 (Ch) (23 March 2005)
http://www.bailii.org/cgi-bin/markup.cgi?doc=/ew/cases/EWHC/Ch/2005/472.html

---

The difficulty in applying fair dealing for the purposes of criticism or review in photographs is that it is difficult to determine what is less than the substantial part of a photograph. It is not as if one can quote briefly from an image as in the case of text. The unauthorized use of a general news photograph of a significant current event is not capable of receiving a fair dealing defence. You cannot use it without permission/remuneration to copyright owner, which is likely to be a professional photographer represented by an agency. You cannot 'help yourself' to images from the Internet – even on historical subjects. Generally in the UK all images taken after July 1912 could have IP/copyright issues. This is true of charities, museums etc. The date is determined by legislation.

✳   A downloadable sound file discussing 'fair dealing' in greater detail and how it relates to images/photographs.
6.2 podcast downloadable https://soundcloud.com/comparativemedialaw/podcast-6-2-the-uk-media-law

6.3 COPYRIGHT DURATION AND MULTIPLE COPYRIGHT INTERESTS IN MEDIA PRODUCTIONS

Novelists, playwrights, composers, artists and poets have copyright in their works during their lifetimes and 70 years *post mortem* – after their deaths. (Rights are often administered by their heirs.) Poetry in particular can be a problem in 'fair dealing'. One or two memorable lines can constitute the substantial part. This is also true of musical lyrics. Some poets' estates are very reluctant to allow quotation for review and criticism without payment. Any arrangement of the poetry into music, drama, publication etc does not amount to review/criticism. Use of any music is likely to have primary and secondary copyright issues: composer, musician, arranger, music publisher and music production company. This is also true of films.

✳   A downloadable sound file briefly covering copyright duration and multiple IP rights in media production.
6.3 podcast downloadable https://soundcloud.com/comparativemedialaw/podcast-6-3-the-uk-media-law

6.4 SOCIAL MEDIA AND NEW DIGITAL PLATFORMS

Social networking content is likely to have copyright issues. Content and images will belong to original owners, even if they have clicked 'public' access protocols. Some social networking sites, e.g. Facebook, claim their own publication copyright. Remember there is no fair dealing immunity in photographs for the purpose of reporting current events. Twitter text content may be regarded as public domain by the licence of agreement between Twitter members and Twitter. But there will not be reporting current events fair dealing rights on Twitpics photographs and images distributed by Twitter messaging.

In December 2012 the UK government published a report on modernizing copyright. It signalled its intention to introduce reforms that would make it legal for private copying for own use, and for research and private study, make educational use of copyright material more simple and flexible, and introduce a fair dealing for 'quotation' and parody and satire. It is intended that private copying should extend to digital online cloud storage, but strictly exclude sharing with other people. It is intended that the copying for parody, caricature and pastiche defence will be limited and maintain the current system of moral rights so that rights holders can object to derogatory treatment. The 'quotation' defence may be a way of ensuring a protected use of short extracts and titles when reporting current events and criticism or review, and use of some 'headline' intrinsic information in online hyperlinks.

> Modernising Copyright: A modern, robust and flexible framework; Government response to consultation on copyright exceptions and clarifying copyright law
> http://www.ipo.gov.uk/response-2011-copyright-final.pdf

★   A downloadable sound file briefly summarizing copyright issues in relation to social media.
6.4 podcast downloadable https://soundcloud.com/comparativemedialaw/podcast-6-4-the-uk-media-law

6.5 ARTWORK, PUBLIC SCULPTURE AND EXHIBITIONS

You may be in a position where you are reviewing/criticizing a public gallery exhibition. You would then usually have permission to film/photograph or use images provided for the purposes of reporting the current event of reviewing the exhibition. Artwork in private spaces is not in public. This could also be true of visual works exhibited in buildings open to the public without an admission charge. Artwork, photographs and sculptures in public places can be photographed and are not usually covered by copyright protection. Hence there is no copyright in taking a photograph of sculpture commissioned for permanent public exhibition in a street. There is no copyright in a photograph of a building taken from a public place.

✳   A downloadable sound file briefly summarizing UK copyright in relation to exhibitions, public sculpture and architecture.
6.5 Podcast downloadable https://soundcloud.com/comparativemedialaw/podcast-6-5-the-uk-media-law

6.6 UPDATES AND STOP PRESS

The companion website page for this chapter contains further detailed briefings, summaries of the case histories referred to, and updates on the subject. A chapter comparing IP law of the UK, USA, Germany and France from *Comparative Media Law and Ethics* published by Routledge in 2009 is podcast downloadable at:

https://soundcloud.com/comparativemedialaw/
chapter12copyrightandintellect

✳   A downloadable sound file updating on key developments in UK copyright and intellectual property law.
6.6 podcast downloadable https://soundcloud.com/comparativemedialaw/podcast-6-6-the-uk-media-law

7

LAWS AND RULES FOR ELECTIONS AND POLITICS

Key bullet points on UK media law when covering elections and politics:

- Normal primary and secondary media law in relation to libel, privacy, accuracy and fairness applies in the coverage of elections
- There is a separate criminal offence for making or publishing a false statement of fact about the personal character or conduct of an election candidate with a purpose to affect the voting
- No qualified privilege for libel applies to candidates' election addresses, but it still adheres to election debates and hustings when they are public meetings and press conferences
- There is a ban on 'exit polls' measuring how people are voting between the beginning and close of polling day – when the electorate casts their votes
- The ban does not apply to the publication of opinion polls on voter intentions before polling begins

- Print and online publishers can be partial and politically biased in favour of candidates and parties
- Licensed UK broadcasters and the BBC have a statutory duty to be impartial and balanced in their coverage of the campaign for election periods
- This requires offering candidates and their parties the opportunity to participate in all reports and programmes covering the election
- Broadcast presenters are not permitted to express their support for any candidate or party in an election or referendum

★ A downloadable sound file vocalizing key bullet points on the media law of UK elections.
7.0 podcast downloadable https://soundcloud.com/comparativemedialaw/chapter-7-bullet-points-the-uk

A short video-cast on the key UK media law points relating to covering elections and politics
7. video-cast http://youtu.be/_WvddYLSkWk

7.1   COVERAGE OF THE CAMPAIGN

The operation of an election or referendum campaign does not suspend or amend existing primary or secondary media law so the coverage of 'hustings' when open and accessible to the public will come under the libel defence of qualified privilege subject to explanation or contradiction for public meetings and press conferences. No qualified privilege will attach to the election addresses distributed by candidates. Extreme political rhetoric that strays into the area of stirring up racial hatred or hatred on religious grounds and gender discrimination are offences under the Racial and Religious Hatred Act 2006, and Public Order Act 1986. The offence of glorifying terrorism arises out of the Terrorism Act 2006.

False statements about candidates with the purpose of impacting on the election constitute a separate criminal offence under section 106(1) of the Representation of the People Act 1983:

http://www.legislation.gov.uk/ukpga/1983/2/section/106

It is unusual though not unknown for the offence to be prosecuted against the media though its construction certainly has a frame that could include publishers:

> A person who, or any director of any body or association corporate which, before or during an election, for the purpose of affecting the return of any candidate at the election, makes or publishes any false statement of fact in relation to the candidate's personal character or conduct shall be guilty of an illegal practice, unless he can show that he had reasonable grounds for believing, and did believe, that statement to be true.

Consent by the candidate against whom the false statement has been made, or his/her agent, is a potential defence and the trial issue would be decided by an Election Court, which can impose a maximum fine of £5,000.

★ A downloadable sound file summarizing primary and secondary media law when covering an election campaign. 7.1 podcast downloadable https://soundcloud.com/comparativemedialaw/podcast-7-1-the-uk-media-law

7.2 IMPARTIALITY RULES FOR BROADCASTERS

A key difference between UK print, magazine and Internet stand-alone publishers and broadcasters is that the former can be partial and party political supporting. Statutory law imposes a duty on all broadcasters to be impartial during election and referendum campaign periods – usually running from the date and time nominations for candidates close. The UK electoral commission (http://

www.electoralcommission.org.uk) is responsible for applying the law of elections and politics to the UK system and publishes detailed guides for the media as well as politicians, their agents, campaigning officials and parties:

> http://www.electoralcommission.org.uk/news-and-media
> Ofcom regulates the compliance of the UK broadcast media to media election law requirements under section 6 of the Broadcasting Code:
> http://stakeholders.ofcom.org.uk/broadcasting/broadcast-codes/broadcast-code/elections/
> Ofcom provides a Guidance briefing on applying the code so that there are practical suggestions on how impartiality can be achieved:
> http://stakeholders.ofcom.org.uk/binaries/broadcast/guidance/831193/section6.pdf

For example if a candidate takes part in an item about his/her constituency then the broadcaster must ensure that each of the major parties is offered an opportunity to take part, as well as those with 'evidence of significant previous or current electoral support'. It would be wise to keep a record of emails and contacts demonstrating evidence of making the offer. The guidance and rule would also suggest that non-significant-support candidates – those on the fringe and seen as representing minority political opinion – do not have to be included in the invitation round. Their presence in the election should be marked by 'best practice that on every occasion that a constituency (or electoral area) report/discussion/debate takes place on radio a full list of candidates standing should be given for that constituency (with a similar provision for referendums)'. This device in television can be achieved by way of screen graphics. Broadcasters' companion online websites can play a rounded role in demonstrating and delivering the duty to impartiality. The detailed reportage of election candidates starts after the close of nominations. The beginning of 'election and referendum periods' is defined in section 6 in relation to the various genres of electoral processes.

You will not be surprised that the BBC Editorial Guidelines under section 10 'Politics, Public Policy and Polls' are extensive:

http://www.bbc.co.uk/guidelines/editorialguidelines/page/
guidelines-politics-practices-elections/
Mandatory referrals are set out at:
http://www.bbc.co.uk/guidelines/editorialguidelines/page/
guidelines-politics-mandatory-referrals/

The BBC, like all broadcasters, is obliged to have regard to any views expressed by the Electoral Commission. All BBC journalists covering elections have the advantage that election and referendum guidelines for TV, radio and online coverage, including message boards, 'will be drawn up by Chief Adviser Politics, agreed by the BBC Trust and published before each campaign'.

Particular care needs to be taken by producers and presenters of live phone-in discussion programmes so as to avoid the expression of any personal support for candidates and parties. Ofcom and a previous regulatory body have imposed penalties when presenters have made off-the-cuff expressions of partiality:

Broadcast Bulletin Issue number 123 – 8 December 2008, The James
Whale Show, Talksport, 20 March 2008, 22:00
http://stakeholders.ofcom.org.uk/enforcement/broadcast-bulletins/
obb123/

In 2000 the previous regulatory body for radio 'The Radio Authority' imposed a fine on the then Virgin Radio presenter and proprietor Chris Evans for expressing political support for Ken Livingstone as a mayoral candidate in London.

http://news.bbc.co.uk/1/hi/entertainment/750646.stm

★ A downloadable sound file setting out the secondary media law rules concerning political impartiality for broadcasters during election campaigns.
7.2 Podcast downloadable https://soundcloud.com/comparativemedialaw/podcast-7-2-the-uk-media-law

7.3   COVERAGE OF POLLING DAY, COUNTING AND RESULT

A key election law issue that applies to all publishers and communicators is the prohibition on exit polls during the period people are voting on polling day. This is set out in section 66A of the Representation of the People Act 1983:

> http://www.legislation.gov.uk/ukpga/1983/2/section/66A/2006–12–01

The law applies to collecting information from voters when they are voting on polling day and publishing the results while the polling continues. The section states:

> No person shall, in the case of an election [...] publish before the poll is closed any statement relating to the way in which voters have voted at the election where that statement is (or might reasonably be taken to be) based on information given by voters after they have voted, or any forecast as to the result of the election which is (or might reasonably be taken to be) based on information so given.

The poll usually closes at 10 p.m. The legislation does not prevent the publication of opinion polls about voters' intentions prior to polling. This means that media publishers can analyse and publish the result of opinion polls on the morning of the polling day. Section 66 of the legislation seeks to protect the secrecy of the voting process and creates criminal offences for anyone seeking and soliciting how people voted in the polling stations.

The Association of Chief Police Officers and the Electoral Commission have also published an online 'Guidance on preventing and detecting electoral malpractice':

> http://www.acpo.police.uk/documents/crime/2011/20110315%20 CBA%20Preventing%20and%20Detecting%20Electoral%20 Malpractice%20Revision%20Feb2011.pdf

It is advisable for media publishers covering elections to establish contact with the returning officers and Electoral Commission teams running and supervising the relevant election/referendum. Applications to have media teams/representatives present at the count and declaration centre should be made as early as possible. In the twenty-first century new digital technologies and the introduction of electronic counting and use of the Internet is liberating the scale and speed of releasing counting and results. This makes the reporting process faster and more accurate and offers greater democratic accessibility. It is important to respect the power and authority of the returning officer and when an election count is by the traditional paper ballot examination and counting process every effort should be made to understand what the boundaries are in relation to what the media representatives present can report before the declaration of the result. Traditionally, returning officers would tolerate journalists doing live broadcasts with candidates indicating that they are 'not expecting to win', without reference and visual publication of the relative size of polling papers for each candidate. But the tracking of detailed electronic counting changes this situation.

★ A downloadable sound file on the media law relating to the coverage of polling day counting and the declaration of results.
7.3 podcast downloadable https://soundcloud.com/comparativemedialaw/podcast-7-3-the-uk-media-law

7.4 UPDATES AND STOP PRESS

The companion website page for this chapter contains further detailed briefings, summaries of the case histories referred to, and updates on the subject.

http://www.ma-radio.gold.ac.uk/mediapocket/chapter7

Updates are also summarized in a stop press podcast.

★   A downloadable sound file updating any developments on the
     media laws and rules for UK elections and politics.
     7.4 podcast downloadable https://soundcloud.com/
     comparativemedialaw/podcast-7-4-the-uk-media-law

8

THE SECRET WORLD

Six bullet points summarizing key laws and concepts affecting the media when covering the secret world:

- The Official Secrets Act 1989 (OSA) is aggressive legislation that is a potential threat to journalists gathering information about security and intelligence stories
- The UK government succeeds in deterring and silencing security and intelligence sources. David Shayler and Keogh and O'Connor cases
- Releasing information the intelligence agencies are reluctant to surrender is hard fought in the courts. Binyam Mohamed case
- Terrorist suspect issues processed from secretive Special Immigration Appeals (SIAC) hearings. Alphabet Soup and terrorist suspect cases
- Stringent proposals for secret hearings in national security proceedings are continually 'on the table'

- The Defence, Press and Broadcasting Advisory Committee (DPBAC) oversees a voluntary code which operates between the UK government departments and defence/security bodies that have responsibilities for national security and the media

★ A downloadable sound file of bullet points summarizing legal issues when covering defence, security and intelligence. 8.0 Podcast downloadable https://soundcloud.com/comparativemedialaw/chapter-8-bullet-points-the-uk

> A short video-cast on the key UK media law points about covering issues of state secrecy.
> 8. video-cast http://youtu.be/MtAbRSMqIoY

8.1   OFFICIAL SECRETS ACT RISKS

Section 5 of the Official Secrets Act 1989 makes it clear that a journalist commits an offence if he/she discloses information, without lawful authority, knowing or having reasonable cause to believe that it is protected against disclosure. The journalist must have received the information from a crown servant or government contractor without lawful authority or in confidence. The journalist can still be prosecuted if he/she received the information from a middle party. The prosecution has to prove that the information was damaging and that the journalist knew it was damaging. The following classes of information are protected by the Act: (1) security and intelligence, (2) defence, (3) international relations, (4) crime, (5) information on government phone-tapping, interception of letters or other communications, and (6) information entrusted in confidence to other states or international organizations.

Section 8 makes it an offence to fail to comply with an 'official' order to return a document, where it would be an offence under the Act if the document were disclosed. The DPP has identified other potential offences under the OSA in sections 1(1), 1(3), 3, 4 and 6.

> UK Official Secrets Act 1989
> http://www.legislation.gov.uk/ukpga/1989/6/contents

In practice the UK state has tended to prosecute civil servants and intelligence officers who have decided to be 'whistle-blowers'. But it is sometimes ranged against journalists. The Metropolitan Police sought a production order using potential OSA offence justification against the *Guardian* in its coverage of police enquiries into phone hacking by News International in 2012 until it backed off as a result of political criticism.

Sometimes prosecution of whistle-blowers such as Foreign Office official Derek Pasquill (2008) and GCHQ translator Katharine Gun (2004) are not successful when their motivation is successfully presented in terms of conscience or the fact that the information is already in the public domain.

> Mr Pasquill was alleged to have breached the OSA by leaking letters and memos about the government's attitude to secret CIA rendition flights and contacts with Muslim groups.
> http://www.guardian.co.uk/media/2008/jan/09/pressandpublishing.freedomofinformation
> Katharine Gun leaked an email about spying on UN diplomats before the UK US invasion of Iraq in 2003.
> http://www.guardian.co.uk/politics/2004/feb/26/interviews.iraq

But other prosecutions of intelligence officers such as David Shayler (MI5) and Cabinet Office communications officer David Keogh and Leo O'Connor, the House of Commons researcher who received the classified document, led to conviction and imprisonment. The document Mr Keogh leaked was a memo on a discussion between US President George W. Bush and UK Prime Minister Tony Blair. The Appeal Court said: 'The meeting was primarily concerned with UK and US policy in Iraq. The discussions concerned current political, diplomatic and defence issues of a highly sensitive nature.' The English courts have issued and sustained reporting bans prohibiting speculation about the memo's contents.

Law Lords' rejection of David Shayler's application for public interest and necessity defence
Shayler, R v [2002] UKHL 11 (21st March, 2002) http://www.bailii.org/uk/cases/UKHL/2002/11.html
Court of Appeal sustaining reporting ban on contents of memo leaked in OSA prosecution
Times Newspapers Ltd & Ors v R [2007] EWCA Crim 1925 (30 July 2007) http://www.bailii.org/ew/cases/EWCA/Crim/2007/1925.html

---

✭   A downloadable sound file exploring the risks to journalists of prosecution under the Official Secrets Act 1989.
8.1 Podcast downloadable https://soundcloud.com/comparativemedialaw/podcast-8-1-the-uk-media-law

8.2   HOW THE BRITISH STATE FIGHTS TOOTH AND NAIL TO KEEP EMBARRASSING INTELLIGENCE MATTERS SECRET AND LEGAL PROCEEDINGS RELATING TO SUSPECT TERRORISTS ARE SMOTHERED IN RESTRICTIONS

The British state uses every legal power it has to maintain what it describes as the interests of 'national security' and media/journalists' attempts to open up serious litigation alleging wrongdoing by the intelligence agencies are very hard fought. Binyam Mohamed, a UK resident, took legal actions alleging UK intelligence were complicit with the US Central Intelligence Agency in relation to his claim that he was unlawfully abducted from Pakistan, subject to rendition and tortured in Morocco. The UK government wanted the details of his allegations suppressed and in particular information supplied from the USA, but the Court of Appeal resisted and released 'redacted' paragraphs in early 2010, largely because the information had already been put into the public domain in the USA by a federal court judge ruling.

> *Mohamed, R (on the application of) v Secretary of State for Foreign &*
> *Commonwealth Affairs* [2010] EWCA Civ 65 (10 February 2010)
> http://www.bailii.org/ew/cases/EWCA/Civ/2010/65.html

Most terrorist suspects processed through the immigration infrastructure of appeal (SIAC) are subject to statutory anonymity orders and restrictions are imposed on how much the media can report their cases. An appeal to the Supreme Court in early 2010 appeared to achieve a victory on the open justice principle. It was known as the 'Alphabet Soup' case.

> *Guardian News and Media Ltd & Ors, Re HM Treasury v Ahmed & Ors*
> [2010] UKSC 1 (27 January 2010)
> http://www.bailii.org/uk/cases/UKSC/2010/1.html

However, in a later case a man subject to a 'control order' because of his suspected involvement in terrorist-related activities had his anonymity sustained when his lawyer submitted: 'There is organised racist activity in the town which has achieved not insignificant local support. There have been racist attacks, including physical violence, on members of the Muslim community in the town. There have also been attempts by racist groups to associate Muslims with terrorism.'

> *Secretary of State for the Home Department v AP (No. 2)* [2010] UKSC
> 26 (23 June 2010)
> http://www.bailii.org/uk/cases/UKSC/2010/26.html

The statutory power provided for SIAC anonymity is set out in SIAC Rule 39(5)h giving it the power to 'make provision to secure the anonymity of the appellant or a witness'.

http://www.legislation.gov.uk/uksi/2003/1034/made

At the time of writing the UK government was processing a Justice and Security Bill with a proposal for 'Closed Material Procedure' (CMP) that would enable the government or intelligence agencies to apply for *in camera*-style hearings in litigation touching on national security issues. Sensitive intelligence issues in legal proceedings tended in the past to be protected by government ministers issuing 'public interest immunity certificates', which would be evaluated by the judges presiding over the case. But the UK intelligence agencies argue that in order to contest a growing amount of terrorism and secret service-related litigation, the closed material procedure would enable the state to present evidence they need to keep secret while the claimants' position would be assisted through the use of special advocates who could not instruct the claimants about the evidence to be concealed. It is argued that this will avoid a tendency for the UK government to surrender to multi-million pound settlements. The Bill also legislates for the parliamentary oversight of state intelligence and security activities.

UK Justice and Security Bill before the House of Lords May 2012
http://www.publications.parliament.uk/pa/bills/lbill/2012–2013/0027/
13027.pdf

The UK courts have a statutory power under section 8(4) of the 1920 version of the Official Secrets Act to exclude the press and public by conducting their proceedings *in camera* on the grounds of national security. All UK courts have a common law power to sit in private (also known as *in chambers*) only if it is possible to serve the administration of justice by doing so and there is no other device or order that could be deployed to maintain the principle of open justice. The leading open justice precedent was the matrimonial dispute of Scott v Scott in 1913. The media can appeal against Crown Court decisions to impose restrictions and exclude the media and public under section 159 of the Administration of Justice Act 1988, and they have the right to apply for judicial review at the High Court in relation to media bans and exclusion in most other court proceedings. Appeals against media exclusion at the Crown Court must be heard by paper submissions and without an oral hearing.

Statutory appeal against reporting restrictions and exclusion of media in relation to trials on indictment (crown court cases)
http://www.legislation.gov.uk/ukpga/1988/33/section/159
The Criminal Procedure Rules 2012, Part 16, Reporting and Access Restrictions:
http://www.justice.gov.uk/courts/procedure-rules/criminal/docs/crim-proc-rules-2012-part-16.pdf
The Criminal Procedure Rules 2012 Part 69 Appeal to the Court of Appeal (criminal division) regarding reporting or public access restriction
http://www.justice.gov.uk/courts/procedure-rules/criminal/docs/crim-proc-rules-2012-part-69.pdf
Successful appeal against holding bail applications in the Crown Court *in chambers*: Malik v Central Criminal Court & Anor [2006] EWHC 1539 (Admin) (27 June 2006)
http://www.bailii.org/ew/cases/EWHC/Admin/2006/1539.html
Unsuccessful challenge to appeal decision without a hearing to hold part of a trial *in camera*: A & Ors, R v [2006] EWCA Crim 4 (13 January 2006)
http://www.bailii.org/ew/cases/EWCA/Crim/2006/4.html
Influential open justice precedent: Scott & Anor v Scott [1913] UKHL 2 (5 May 1913)
http://www.bailii.org/uk/cases/UKHL/1913/2.html
Section 8(4) Official Secrets Act 1920
www.legislation.gov.uk/ukpga/Geo5/10-11/75/section/8
Successful appeal against 'closed material procedure' during civil litigation: Al Rawi & Ors v The Security Service & Ors [2011] UKSC 34 (13 July 2011)
http://www.bailii.org/uk/cases/UKSC/2011/

★ A downloadable sound file discussing the tension between open and secret justice in relation to national security and intelligence cases.
8.2 Podcast downloadable https://soundcloud.com/comparativemedialaw/podcast-8-2-the-uk-media-law

8.3   DEFENCE, PRESS AND BROADCASTING ADVISORY COMMITTEE

The UK benefits from a liaison body, set up in 1912 – and the same year as the British Board of Film Censorship – that seeks to negotiate between state military and security intelligence bodies and the media to ensure that publications do not jeopardize the lives of service-people. In 2012 it has evolved to the extent that there are standing Defence Advisory Notices that any journalist or publisher can consult online for advice.

```
http://www.dnotice.org.uk/danotices/index.htm
```

A full-time 'two-star' equivalent general, admiral or air marshal operates in an advisory role with out-of-office-hours access. The DPBAC is unique in the world for the cooperation achieved between state security and media publication bodies. It has certainly benefited from much respected full-time secretaries such as Air Vice Marshal Andrew Vallance and his predecessor Rear-Admiral Nicholas Wilkinson. In its pledge to support the principles of freedom of information and transparency the committee declares:

> Although not subject to the Freedom of Information Act 2000 or the Freedom of Information (Scotland) Act of 2002, the DPBAC is committed to practising a policy of maximum disclosure of its activities consistent with the effective conduct of business and the need to ensure that it honours any assurance of confidentiality given to the individuals and organisations with which it deals.

What that means is that journalists are able to consult the Secretary to obtain important indications of whether any information about to be published would be regarded as damaging to national security and in particular why the lives of service and intelligence personnel could be threatened. Furthermore, their stories would not be compromised and given away to the competition, which is the likely fate with public releases under the Freedom of Information Act.

The Defence Advisory (DA) Notice system
http://www.dnotice.org.uk/

✱   A downloadable sound file briefly summarizing the
    operation of the Defence, Press and Broadcasting, Advisory
    Committee.
    8.3 podcast downloadable https://soundcloud.com/
    comparativemedialaw/podcast-8-3-the-uk-media-law

8.4 UPDATES AND STOP PRESS

The companion website page for this chapter contains further
detailed briefings, summaries of the case histories referred to, and
updates on the subject.

http://www.ma-radio.gold.ac.uk/mediapocket/chapter8

The BBC Editorial Guidelines contain a very useful briefing
on its referral policy and frame of standards when reporting and
covering 'War, Terror and Emergencies, National Security and
Counter Terrorism':

http://www.bbc.co.uk/editorialguidelines/page/
guidelines-war-practices-security/

Updates are also summarized in a stop press podcast.

✱   A downloadable sound file updating developments in relation
    to media law and state security.
    8.4 podcast downloadable https://soundcloud.com/
    comparativemedialaw/podcast-8-4-updates-and-stop

9

SCOTTISH AND NORTHERN IRISH DIFFERENCES AND ISSUES

Bullet points summarizing some key differences in the media law of Scotland and Northern Ireland:

- Scotland and Northern Ireland have separate legal systems, with the Scottish jurisdiction having substantially different traditions, influences, rituals and terminology
- There are signs the judiciary in Scotland and Northern Ireland are more sensitive to aggressive criticism that is construed as contemptuous
- Juries in Scotland are 15 with majorities possible to 8–7 and a third 'not proven' verdict
- In Scotland, publication of images/photographs of accused people is usually regarded as potential contempt of court because of the legal doctrine of 'dock identification'
- There are no youth/juvenile courts in Scotland and young people aged 16 and under investigated for criminal offences are dealt with by a children's panel system

usually sitting in private with legal restrictions on their identity; it is possible to identify young people aged 17 when appearing in the adult courts in Scotland

- All sexual offence complainants in courts in Scotland and Northern Ireland receive similar forms of protection in terms of anonymity for life and are not identified
- Scottish criminal courts close the public gallery but permit the presence of reporters when alleged victims of sexual offences give their evidence
- In Northern Ireland courts are willing to permit anonymity for criminal defendants if there is evidence that identification will undermine their right to life because of the risk of vigilante attacks

☆ A downloadable sound file of bullet points highlighting some key differences in the media law of Scotland and Northern Ireland.
9.0 podcast downloadable https://soundcloud.com/comparativemedialaw/chapter-9-bullet-points-uk

A short video-cast explaining some key differences and issues in the media law of Northern Ireland and Scotland.
9. video-cast http://youtu.be/P_wqCS4XUwc

9.1 KEY SCOTTISH DIFFERENCES

When there was political and constitutional union between Scotland and England in 1707 it did not include a fusion of the countries' legal systems. Consequently the fact there has been a separate jurisdiction in Scotland for many centuries means that there are many differences in ritual, structure, court practice and traditions. Scottish law is much more heavily influenced by the Roman civil law doctrine. The BBC's College of Journalism has an excellent online summary of the structural differences:

'Reporting court cases in Scotland'
http://www.bbc.co.uk/academy/collegeofjournalism/law/courts/
reporting-court-cases-in-scotland
As previously indicated in this book, the Scottish government also
provides detailed online explanations of its separate legal system in
'Courts and the Legal System'
http://www.scotland.gov.uk/Topics/Justice/legal

The Human Rights Act 1998 is probably the most cohesive framework of legislation establishing parity between England and Wales and Scotland. For example it might be argued that it had the effect of making the application of media contempt law in Scotland less severe by directing the Scottish judges to balance Article 10 freedom of expression with Article 6, the right to fair trial.

Scotland recently raised the age of criminal responsibility from eight to twelve to bring it in line with the majority of European countries in contrast to the position in England and Wales where it remains ten. This was achieved by section 52 of the Criminal Justice and Licensing (Scotland) Act 2010 (http://www.legislation.gov.uk/asp/2010/13/section/52). This is an example of statutes that are unique to Scotland and of course, its legal system's separate customs and case law are applicable to any understanding or application of media law there. The companion website provides much more detail about the Scottish system and case histories, but it is useful to appreciate some of the key differences. Brief reference has been made to the fact that criminal juries consist of 15 people, there are no prosecution opening speeches and the legal ritual involves the use of unique terminology. For example, the criminal defendant at trial is referred to as 'the panel' and not the accused.

Children in Scotland investigated for crimes (aged 16 and under) are not tried through a criminal courts system such as the Youth Courts, previously known as juvenile courts. There is a much more social-worker-orientated approach and anonymity powers and restrictions operate with equal severity whether children appear as witnesses, parties before the special children's panels or elsewhere in the legal system.

Section 47 of the Criminal Procedure (Scotland) Act 1995
http://www.legislation.gov.uk/ukpga/1995/46/section/47
Section 46 of the Children and Young Persons (Scotland) Act 1937
http://www.legislation.gov.uk/ukpga/Edw8and1Geo6/1/37/section/46

In criminal cases, because of the formal legal process of dock identification, it is normally considered a contempt of court to publish photographs/images of an accused person before the Crown has completed its case at trial. There may be rare exceptions where an accused is so widely known because of his or her public profile, but you must take specialist advice from Scottish media law experts. Potential cross-border publication between Northern Ireland, Scotland, and England and Wales must respect the particular jurisdictional issues for each legal system where there might be a national police enquiry with trials and indictments relating to the same people in the different countries. This would be true, for example, of a serial killer whose crimes were distributed throughout the UK.

Sexual offence complainants in Scotland receive the protection of the law though by different mechanisms. It is wise to assume a default position of lifetime anonymity from the time a complaint is made until such time that any indication of a waiver or court direction that identification is permissible is confirmed by specialist legal advice. The Scottish media have a much more ethical reputation and background in working with the judiciary to operate a reliable custom and practice of not identifying sexual offence complainants while they give their evidence in criminal trials with the presence of reporters but exclusion of the public. This process is backed up with statutory and case law powers namely:

Sexual Offences Amendment Act 1992 extended to Scotland in 2004
http://www.legislation.gov.uk/ssi/2004/408/article/3/made
Section 90 of the Criminal Justice and Licensing (Scotland Act) 2010
http://www.legislation.gov.uk/asp/2010/13/section/90
Section 92(3) of the Criminal Procedure (Scotland) Act 1995
http://www.legislation.gov.uk/ukpga/1995/46/section/92

It should also be appreciated that the judiciary in Scotland and Northern Ireland may not be as tolerant as their counterparts in England and Wales of criticism of their decisions and judicial role particularly if it is perceived as contemptuous. A solicitor in Scotland had to address the charge about his post-trial comments to the media as recently as 2008:

Anwar, Re Possible Contempt Of Court [2008] ScotHC HCJAC_36 (01 July 2008)
http://www.bailii.org/scot/cases/ScotHC/2008/HCJAC_36.html
The British politician, Peter Hain, was also accused of being legally contemptuous to a senior member of the Northern Ireland judiciary, but the case did not proceed:
Peter Hain contempt charge dropped [...] lawyers query offence of 'scandalising a judge'
http://www.guardian.co.uk/politics/2012/may/17/
peter-hain-contempt-case-dropped

A debate continues about whether the judges should be robust enough to weather the storm of the rough and tumble of criticism they regard as unwarranted and without justification.

✻   A downloadable sound file highlighting some key Scottish media law issues.
    9.1 podcast downloadable https://soundcloud.com/comparativemedialaw/podcast-9-1-uk-media-law

9.2 KEY NORTHERN IRELAND DIFFERENCES

The legal system of Northern Ireland is much more similar to England and Wales than could be said of that of Scotland. The province has its own judiciary and there are separate powers derived from statutory instruments in the form of orders from the Secretary of State for Northern Ireland. Significant case law and statutory instruments are explored in greater detail on the companion website.

The Judicial Studies Board for Northern Ireland (JSB) is an excellent resource on the specific legal issues, practices, and structures operating there:

> http://www.jsbni.com/Pages/default.aspx
> The JSB has very helpfully produced a detailed and comprehensive online guide to reporting restrictions:
> http://www.jsbni.com/Publications/reporting-restrictions/Pages/default.aspx

The historical background of sectarian conflict resulted in the operation of judge-only 'Diplock' courts for terrorist-related crimes, but the Good Friday Agreement and a long period of stability and peace mean that non-jury criminal trials are rarer than they used to be. However, the real risk that existed to people serving as jurors and the continuation of vigilante threats of violence by paramilitary groups means that courts in Northern Ireland are more anxious to protect people selected for jury service and criminal defendants who fear for their safety. It is a specific criminal offence to identify anyone as having done jury service, to be actually serving as a juror or to have been included in a panel selected for potential jury service:

> Article 26 of the Juries (Northern Ireland) Order 1996 (S.I. 1996/1141 (N.I. 6)
> http://www.legislation.gov.uk/nisi/1996/1141/article/26A
> The protection is further consolidated in section 10 of the Justice and Security (Northern Ireland) Act 2007
> http://www.legislation.gov.uk/ukpga/2007/6/crossheading/juries

The media in Northern Ireland are alert to asserting the open justice principle and case law indicates that the judiciary engage acute issues in balancing freedom of expression and open justice with the administration of justice and human rights of participants in legal proceedings.

In a case in 2009 the Court of Appeal, the highest court in Northern Ireland, ruled on an application that witnesses to an enquiry should not be named and identified as former soldiers:

> *A & Ors, Re Judicial Review* [2009] NICA 6 (11 February 2009)
> http://www.bailii.org/nie/cases/NICA/2009/6.html

In 2011, the court ruled on an application by a former politician that an application for the continuation of an injunction on privacy issues should be heard in private.

> *Robinson v Sunday Newspapers Ltd* [2011] NICA 13 (25 May 2011)
> http://www.bailii.org/nie/cases/NICA/2011/13.html

There is a system of youth courts in Northern Ireland with the criminal age of responsibility set at ten and anonymity restrictions on young people similar to the situation in England and Wales. There are powers to exclude both the press and public from criminal proceedings where children give evidence about sexual crimes and issues.

★   A downloadable sound file highlighting some media law
     issues specific to Northern Ireland.
     9.2 podcast downloadable https://soundcloud.com/
     comparativemedialaw/podcast-9-2-the-uk-media-law

9.3   UPDATES AND STOP PRESS

The companion website page for this chapter contains further detailed briefings, summaries of the case histories referred to, and updates on the subject.

> http://www.ma-radio.gold.ac.uk/mediapocket/chapter9

Updates are also summarized in a stop press podcast.

★   A downloadable sound file updating media law developments
     in Scotland and Northern Ireland.
     9.3 podcast downloadable https://soundcloud.com/
     comparativemedialaw/podcast-9-3-the-uk-media-law

INDEX

As this is a pocketbook and not a formal law textbook, cases and statutes are inserted into the index. Acronyms are spelled out, though there is a short acronym system for the case law references:

ECtHR   European Court of Human Rights
UKHL   United Kingdom judicial committee of the House of Lords (until 2010)
HKCFA Hong Kong Court for Appeals
EWHC   England and Wales High Court
EWHC (COP) England and Wales High Court of Protection
EWCA   England and Wales Court of Appeal: Civil Division
EWCC   England and Wales Court of Appeal: Criminal Division
SHCJ   Scottish High Court of Justiciary
NICA   Court of Appeal, Northern Ireland